The TAO *of*
HEALTH,
LONGEVITY, *and*
IMMORTALITY

The TAO of HEALTH, LONGEVITY, and IMMORTALITY

The Teachings of Immortals Chung and Lü

TRANSLATED BY

Eva Wong

Shambhala

BOSTON & LONDON

2000

Shambhala Publications, Inc.
Horticultural Hall
300 Massachusetts Avenue
Boston, Massachusetts 02115
www.shambhala.com

9 8 7 6 5 4 3 2 1

First Edition
Printed in the United States of America

♾ This edition is printed on acid-free paper that meets the
American National Standards Institute Z39.48 Standard.
Distributed in the United States by Random House, Inc.,
and in Canada by Random House of Canada Ltd

Library of Congress Cataloging-in-Publication Data
Chung-Lü ch'uan-tao chi. English.
The Tao of health, longevity, and immortality: the teachings of
immortals Chung and Lü / Translated by Eva Wong.
p.   cm.
ISBN 1-57062-725-8 (alk. paper)
1. Hygiene, Taoist. 2. Lè, Tung-pin, b. 798. 3. Chung-li, Chèän,
9th cent. I. Wong, Eva, 1951– II. Title.
RA781.C5313   2000
613'.0951'09021—dc21
00-040035

Contents

The Tao of Health, Longevity, and Immortality

Translator's Introduction

IMMORTALS CHUNGLI CH'UAN AND LÜ TUNG-PIN

The immortals Chungli Ch'uan and Lü Tung-pin are two of the most popular figures in Taoism and Chinese culture. Most people recognize them as characters belonging to a group called the Eight Immortals—Lü Tung-pin, Chungli Ch'uan, Chang Kuo Lao, Ho Hsien-ku, Han Hsiang Tzu, Ts'ao Kuo-chiu, T'ieh-kuai Li, and Lan Ts'ai-ho. Stories of these eight colorful Taoists have fired the imagination of the Chinese through the centuries: I was familiar with these immortals and their exploits well before I began to study the Taoist texts and practice the Taoist arts.

Of the eight, Lü Tung-pin, Chungli Ch'uan, Ho Hsien-ku, and Chang Kuo Lao had the most impact on the theory and practice of Taoism today. Chungli Ch'uan was an alchemist; along with Wei Po-yang, he is regarded as one of the founders of the alchemical arts of longevity and immortality. Lü Tung-pin was a meditation master and the patriarch of several Taoist sects that included both the northern and the southern schools of Complete Reality Taoism (Ch'üan-chen), the Earlier Heaven Way (Hsien-t'ien Tao), and the Green City sect (Ch'ing-ch'eng) of Szechuan. Ho Hsien-ku was an alchemist and the patron of female Taoist cultivation: many practices of

1

female internal alchemy are attributed to her. Chang Kuo Lao is famous for his work on celestial divination: his system of astrology is still widely studied and used by modern Chinese diviners.

This book is a translation of the text *Chung-Lü ch'uan-tao chi* (The Teachings of the Tao As Transmitted by Chung and Lü). The original text is collected in the *Sung-shi wei-wen chi* (Collected Literary Works of the Sung Dynasty) and is believed to have been written as an introduction to the *Ling-pao pi-fa* (Scripture of the Definitive Methods of the Precious Spirit), a text for advanced practitioners.

The text uses a conversation between Lü Tung-pin and Chungli Ch'uan to present the theory and methods of the art of health, longevity, and immortality. However, historically Chungli Ch'uan lived in the Han dynasty (206 BCE–219 CE) and Lü Tung-pin lived in the latter part of the T'ang (618–906 CE). How can two people who lived almost eight hundred years apart coauthor a book?

I believe that there are two possible answers to this question.

The first is this: they met, and during the encounter, Chungli Ch'uan transmitted his teachings to Lü Tung-pin. This answer is based on the legends and stories of the two immortals.

The second answer is that they never met. Lü Tung-pin took Chungli Ch'uan's teachings and revived and reinterpreted them. This answer is based on the analysis of the historical and philosophical background of the *Chung-Lü ch'uan-tao chi.*

We shall examine the ramifications of each answer in turn.

Two stories stand out in the legends of Chungli Ch'uan and Lü Tung-pin. The first tells of the meeting between the two men. Legend has it that toward the end of the T'ang dynasty, Lü Tung-pin (who was then called Lü Yen) met Chungli Ch'uan when he was on his way to the capital to take the civil service examinations. At that time Lü was an aspiring young man hoping to get an appointment in the government and Chungli was an immortal visiting the mortal realm. The two met at an inn, and after an evening of drinking and talking, Chungli gave Lü a pillow as a parting gift. That night Lü Yen laid his head on the pillow, slept, and had a dream. He dreamed that he took the imperial examinations, passed them with distinction, and became a high-ranking official. However, as the dream unfolded, Lü saw himself embroiled in court politics and intrigues. Eventually, schemed against by unscrupulous and jealous ministers, he was exiled to the frontier, where he died, far from family and home. The next morning Lü woke up and realized that fame, wealth, and social prestige were illusions. He left the inn and followed Chungli Ch'uan into the mountains. Lü Yen, the Confucian scholar, became Lü Tung-pin (Lü, the Guest of the Cavern), the student of the Taoist arts of longevity and immortality. It was said that Lü eventually ascended to immortality after completing his training with Chungli Ch'uan, but before he left the mortal realm, he transmitted his teachings to students who later became teachers and founders of some of the most important Taoist sects today. These students were Wang Ch'ung-yang, the founder of the Northern School of Complete Reality Taoism; Liu Hai-ch'an, the founder of the Southern School of Complete Reality Taoism; and Chen Hsi-yi, the patriarch of the Earlier Heaven Way. Today the practitioners of these sects, as well as those of the Green City sect of Szechuan, all claim Lü Tung-pin as their founding patriarch.

The second story tells of an incident that happened while Lü Tung-pin was studying under Chungli Ch'uan. In this story the elder immortal, Chungli, offered to teach his student the method of turning stones into gold. When Lü realized that the effects were impermanent, he told his teacher that he would rather not learn a technique that could potentially delude or harm people. Chungli Ch'uan then confessed that his student was more "enlightened" than he was and predicted that Lü would surpass him in attaining the Tao.

The first story is most likely an older tale. In it, Lü was portrayed as a deluded intellectual and Chungli was the teacher who "awakened" him from his illusions. The story appears in the literary works of Lü Yen himself, which are believed to have been collected no later than the Sung dynasty (960–1279 CE). In the second story, Lü was still a student but was now recognized to have a stronger understanding of the Tao than his teacher. This story appears in *Seven Taoist Masters*, a novel about the seven students of Wang Ch'ung-yang and the founding of the Northern School of Complete Reality Taoism. The style of the book suggests that it was written no earlier than the Ming dynasty (1368–1644 CE). Thus the second story was written at least four hundred years after the first one.

Much has happened to the status of the immortals Chungli Ch'uan and Lü Tung-pin "between" the two stories. During the Sung and the Ming dynasties, Lü Tung-pin was transformed from student to prominent teacher of the Taoist arts to high-ranking celestial immortal. He was deified and given the titles Shun-yang Ti-chun (Lord Emperor of Pure Yang), Fu-yu Ti-chun (Lord Emperor Protector, the Right Hand Assistant), and Lü-ti (Emperor Lü). Chungli Ch'uan, however, remained Hun-fang Hsien-sheng (Resident of the Cloud Chamber) and was given only the immortal title Cheng-yang Chen-jen (Realized Being of the True Yang). To put it simply, Lü eventually became a celestial immortal, the highest rank of Taoist immortals—he held the title of ti (emperor in the celestial realm)—while Chungli Ch'uan attained only spirit immortality, the level of immortality below celestial immortality; he only held the title of chen-jen (realized being).

Lü's elevation in the community of immortals is evident in the tales surrounding the Eight Immortals. By seniority, Chungli should have been the leader of the group: he was the eldest, having attained immortality in the Han dynasty. The other seven immortals, including Lü Tung-pin, attained immortality during the T'ang and Sung. In order for Lü to end up as the leader of this famous group, he must have attained a higher level of enlightenment than his former teacher Chungli; thus we have the episode related in *Seven Taoist Masters.*

We also see the transformation of Lü Tung-pin from Taoist practitioner to celestial lord in the writings that are attributed to him. These writings clearly fall into two distinct groups. In the first group Lü is identified as either Lü or Lü Tung-pin. These texts are believed to have been written by Lü himself or by his immediate students, before Lü was deified. They include Lü's poetry and the text translated in this book, the *Chung-Lü ch'uan-tao chi.* In the second group of texts, Lü is referred to as Lü Tsu (Patriarch Lü), Shun-yang Ti-chun, and/or Fu-yu Ti-chun. These texts include the *Lü Tsu wu-p'ien* (Five Treatises by Patriarch Lü and their commentaries) and the various liturgies found in the *Lü Tsu ch'uan-shu* (Complete Writings of Patriarch Lü). (This *Lü Tsu ch'uan-shu* was published during the reign of Ch'ing dynasty emperor Ch'ien-lung [1736–1795 CE]. It is *not* the collection of texts with the same title edited recently by Hsiao T'ien-shih of Taiwan.)

Did the historical Lü Tung-pin *really* meet the Han dynasty immortal Chungli Ch'uan? We shall never know. However, regardless of whether they met or not, the teachings of the *Chung-Lü ch'uan-tao chi* are remarkably similar to those taught by the Han dynasty masters of the arts of longevity and immortality. This leads us to the second answer concerning the authorship of the text: that Lü and Chungli never met, and that Lü reinterpreted and revived the teachings of Chungli Ch'uan. To examine the ramifications of this answer, we need to look at the background of the *Chung-Lü ch'uan-tao chi.*

THE HISTORICAL AND PHILOSOPHICAL BACKGROUND OF THE TEXT

Although the text is attributed to both Chungli Ch'uan and Lü Tung-pin, it was probably written by Lü Tung-pin or Lü's students in the Five Dynasties (907–960 CE) or the early part of the Sung dynasty. This makes the *Chung-Lü ch'uan-tao chi* one of the earliest works attributed to Immortal Lü. The text cites another work, the *Ling-pao pi-fa*, which has been identified by Chinese scholars to be a work of the late T'ang or the Five Dynasties period. (Lü himself lived from the end of the T'ang through the Five Dynasties to the early Sung.)

Between the Eastern Han (25–219 CE) (the era of Chungli Ch'uan) and the late T'ang (the period of Lü Tung-pin), the Taoist arts of longevity and immortality went through several major phases of development.

First came the alchemists of the late Han through the Chin (265–420 CE) dynasties—practitioners who tried to compound minerals into a pill that, if ingested, can make a mortal immortal. Many of these alchemists, like Chungli Ch'uan, Wei Po-yang, and Ko Hung, were not only exponents of ingesting pills and elixirs but also adepts in the methods of calisthenics, breath control, meditation, and even sexual yoga. Thus the early Taoist arts of longevity and immorality were a mixture of external alchemy, the method of ingesting pills; sexual alchemy, the method of gathering energy from a sexual partner; and internal alchemy, the method of transforming the body with breath control, calisthenics, and meditation.

Then, in the Chin, came the Shang-ch'ing movement founded by Lady Wei Hua-ts'un. This school introduced the techniques of swallowing saliva, absorbing the essences of nature (sun, moon, stars, fog, mist), and visualizing the guardian deities of the body into the arts of longevity and immortality. The Shang-ch'ing methods were popular throughout the Six Dynasties (420–589 CE), the Sui dynasty (589–618 CE) and the T'ang. However, during the T'ang there was also a revival of external alchemy, the method of attaining immortality by ingesting pills and elixirs. The external alchemy of the T'ang was different from the earlier form practiced by Wei Po-yang and the alchemists of the Han: it did not use sexual yoga, calisthenics, and breath control to complement the practice of ingesting pills. In this latter form of external alchemy, the success of manufacturing the pill of immortality depended on building the alchemical apparatus according to the numerics (or measurements) of the Tao as manifested in nature. Also, during the T'ang, Ssu-ma Ch'eng-ch'en, the great patriarch of Shang-ch'ing Taoism, introduced the method of internal observation (the meditation of internal gazing) into the practices of that school. This form of meditation was soon adopted by other Taoist schools as well.

By the late T'ang, however, the heyday of external alchemy was over. After several centuries of research, the alchemists had failed to produce a pill of immortality. Along with their failures, many, including emperors, had died of lead or mercuric poisoning when they ingested minerals and stones. Also, after the middle T'ang, Ch'an (Zen) and T'ien-tai meditation, which resembles vipassana or insight meditation, began to compete with the Taoist arts of longevity and immortality as methods of spiritual cultivation. Buddhism introduced a "problem" to spiritual cultivation as well as a "solution" to it. The problem was reincarnation; the solution was to get rid of the aggregates (skandhas) that "cause" rebirth; and the method was emptying the mind through meditative stillness. The influence of Buddhism was so pervasive during the T'ang that many Buddhist beliefs were incorporated into Taoism. It is from the late T'ang onward that we begin to see the concepts of reincarnation and karmic retribution appearing in the Taoist texts.

When the T'ang dynasty fell in 906, it was replaced by the Five Dynasties, a period of civil unrest and unstable government. One military coup followed another, and assassinations and brute force became the norm to put emperors on the throne. The Confucian-based civil service was demoralized, and many scholars began to abandon it for Buddhism or Taoism. In this context the story of a young and idealistic Lü Yen becoming disillusioned with politics fits very well with the intellectual atmosphere of the time.

This was the political, social, and intellectual scene that

Lü Yen found himself in during the late T'ang and the Five Dynasties: external alchemy was on the decline, insight and Ch'an meditation were on the rise, the Buddhist idea of reincarnation was beginning to creep into Taoist beliefs, and there was a general disillusionment toward Confucianism and its ability to provide social and political stability. All this was to result in the intellectual community's shifting its focus from social engagement to self-cultivation. Thus, in the late T'ang and Five Dynasties, we find many Confucians becoming Ch'an Buddhists and Taoists. Lü Tung-pin himself was a Confucian scholar before embracing Taoism. Some of Lü's most famous students were either Confucians or Buddhists before they became Taoists. For example, Wang Ch'ung-yang was a Confucian and then a Ch'an Buddhist before becoming a Taoist; Chen Hsi-yi was originally a Confucian; and Liu Hai-ch'an was originally a Ch'an Buddhist. A new approach to cultivating health, longevity, and immortality emerged from the innovative thinking of these teachers. This was internal alchemy—the theory and method of transforming body and mind from within.

Internal alchemy went through three major phases of development between the late T'ang and the present. The early phase of internal alchemy started around the end of the T'ang dynasty and ended at the beginning of the Sung. During this short formative period, the internal alchemists, such as Lü Tung-pin, were not hostile to external alchemy. They merely stated that external alchemy was no longer a viable method. The practitioners also did not consider the "paired practice" of sexual alchemy antagonistic to the "solo practice" of the Singular Path. In fact, texts like the *Chung-Lü ch'uan-tao chi* recommended the use of sexual alchemy for practitioners who started cultivation after middle age. Texts from this period also tried to incorporate the Shang-ch'ing methods of visualization and internal observation into the practice of internal alchemy. Finally, in this period we begin to detect a distinct influence of Buddhism: the Taoist techniques of immortality were presented as a solution to the Buddhist problem of reincarnation.

The next phase of internal alchemy coincided with the Sung dynasty. In the early Sung we begin to see attacks on external alchemy by internal alchemists (for example, see Chang Po-tuan's texts). The attacks even extended to the Shang-ch'ing methods of visualization and absorbing the essences of nature. These hostilities were probably attempts to establish internal alchemy as an independent and premier discipline of Taoist practice. Finally, the "paired practice" of sexual alchemy and the "solo practice" of the Singular Path became separate paths of training. Eventually internal alchemy became identified as the Singular Path and sexual alchemy became identified as the Paired Path.

The third phase of internal alchemy began in the Ming dynasty and extended through the Ch'ing (1644–1911 CE) and the Republican era (1911–1949). During this period many internal-alchemical texts did not even mention external alchemy at all: it is as if the discipline did not exist. Probably this is because, by then, external alchemy was no longer practiced. Attacks on the Shang-ch'ing methods also stopped because, by the Ming, the Shang-ch'ing school ceased to be a distinct lineage. The technique of internal observation, which was the hallmark of Shang-ch'ing practice in the T'ang, has been incorporated into mainstream internal alchemy. (For example, see my *Cultivating the Energy of Life,* a translation of Liu Hua-yang's *Hui-ming ching*).

The *Chung-Lü ch'uan-tao chi* has all the characteristics of a text from the early or formative period of internal alchemy. First, Lü Tung-pin is not identified as a celestial lord in the text. He is simply referred to as Lü; the titles Shun-yang Ti-chun, Fu-yu Ti-chun, or Lü-ti are absent.

Second, the text is very close in spirit to the alchemical texts of the Han dynasty. It is not hostile to external alchemy; in fact, it "apologizes" for the failure of the external pill (see chapter 9). Also, it does not consider paired practice and solo practice antagonistic: the text recommends that older novices use sexual alchemy to gather energy in the early phases of cultivation (see chapter 9). Other than incorporating the Buddhist idea of reincarnation and the Shang-ch'ing techniques of visualization and internal observation, the teachings of the text are remarkably similar to those of the early alchemical classics such as Wei Po-yang's *Tsan-tung-chi* (Triplex Unity) and *Lung-fu ching* (Dragon-Tiger Classic). (For a translation of the Dragon-Tiger Classic, see my *Harmonizing Yin and Yang*.)

Third, the *Chung-Lü ch'uan-tao chi* shows the influence of the external alchemy of the T'ang dynasty. This is evidenced by the fact that the text goes out of its way to demonstrate the parallel workings of the macrocosmos of the Tao in nature and the microcosmos of the Tao in the body (see chapters 3, 4, 5, 6, 9, 11, and 15). The text also argues for the importance of patterning the internal alchemical transformations after the design of the natural world in the same manner as the external alchemists of the T'ang tried to pattern the alchemical equipment after the principles of the Tao as manifested in nature. The struggle to draw parallels between the "numerics" (or measurements) of the human body and the natural world is most obvious in chapters 5, 6, 7, 14, and 15. It appears that the author of the *Chung-Lü ch'uan-tao chi* was reluctant to abandon a paradigm that had not quite disappeared but at the same time wanted to replace it with a new one. By the time of Chang Po-tuan in the early Sung, internal alchemy finally shook off the baggage of the need to draw parallels between the numerics of the human body and the natural world.

Fourth, the text tries to incorporate internal observation and visualization, both Shang-ch'ing techniques, into internal alchemy. This is most evident in chapter 16. By the time of Chang Po-tuan, the technique of visualization was no longer recommended or discussed in the internal-alchemical texts.

The *Chung-Lü ch'uan-tao chi* is one of a handful of texts from the early or formative period of internal alchemy (the other is the *Ling-pao pi-fa*). As such, the text gives us valuable insights into the early phase of internal alchemy: how it struggled to establish itself as a unique spiritual tradition while at the same time being reluctant to break its ties with external alchemy; how it tried to "apologize" for the failure of external alchemy; how it attempted to incorporate the Shang-ch'ing methods of visualization and internal observation; and how it began to synthesize the Taoist art of immortality with the Buddhist ideas of reincarnation and karmic retribution.

While the text shows influences of Buddhism, Shang-ch'ing Taoism, and T'ang dynasty external alchemy, the core of its teachings is remarkably similar to the Taoist alchemical texts of the Han. When we compare the *Chung-Lü ch'uan-tao chi* with the *Tsan-tung-chi* (Triplex Unity) and the *Lung-fu-ching* (Dragon-Tiger Classic), we realize that Lü Tung-pin's understanding of these texts was remarkable; it is almost as if he had directly "received" the teachings from Chungli Ch'uan and the Han dynasty alchemists. Thus, even though Lü and Chungli lived eight hundred years apart and may not have met in real life, it is not unreasonable to acknowledge that Lü Tung-pin was the spiritual successor to Chungli Ch'uan and that the *Chung-Lü ch'uan-tao chi* was "authored" by both of them.

THE MAIN TEACHINGS OF THE *CHUNG-LÜ CH'UAN-TAO CHI*

(For readers who are unfamiliar with the teachings and practice of Taoist internal alchemy, this section can be used as a guide to reading the text.)

The teachings of the text are divided into five topics:

1. What immortality is and how it can be attained by realizing the laws of the Tao within us
2. The arts of health: methods and benefits of the Lesser Path
3. The arts of longevity: methods and benefits of the Middle Path

4. The arts of immortality: methods and benefits of the Great Path

5. How to deal with obstacles and how to recognize spiritual progress

What Immortality Is and How It Can Be Attained by Realizing the Laws of the Tao within Us

There are five types of immortals: ghost, human, earth, spirit, and celestial. Of these, the middle three levels (human, earth, and spirit) are readily attainable. The lowest level of immortality (ghost immortal) is not desirable and the highest level (celestial immortal) is beyond the comprehension of beginning practitioners. (Recall that the *Chung-Lü ch'uan-tao chi* was written for novices.)

Human immortality is achievable by methods of the Lesser Path. These methods can be practiced exclusively for health or used to build foundations for the advanced levels of cultivation. Earth immortality is achievable by methods of the Middle Path and can be practiced to attain longevity. Spirit immortality is achievable by methods of the Great Path and can be practiced to attain immortality.

The earth, sky, sun, and moon can last forever because they follow the natural laws of the Tao. If humans are to live forever, they too must get their bodies to function according to the same laws. The two most important principles of the Tao that are manifested in nature are the rise and fall and the flow and ebb of the yin and yang vapors. The rise and the fall of the vapors anchor the seasons, and their flow and ebb govern the behavior of the moon.

In the human body, the rise and fall of vapor and fluid (two "carriers" of generative energy) are patterned after the cycle of the rise and fall of the yin and yang vapors in nature, and their waxing and waning are patterned after the monthly cycle of the moon. To receive the full benefits of cultivation, practitioners must synchronize their schedule of training with the production and the ascent and descent of vapor and fluid in the body. These topics are discussed in chapters 1 through 6.

Hints for Reading This Section

- Don't get hung up on the numerics of the parallel structures between the human body and the natural world. Many of the numerics are now considered antiquated by practitioners.
- Make sure you understand that the production and movement of the two "carriers" of generative energy—vapor and fluid—follow some sort of biological clock in the body.

The Arts of Health: Methods and Benefits of the Lesser Path

The Lesser Path is concerned with cultivating health. Training in the Lesser Path involves producing mundane generative energy and transforming it into its primordial form. These are the methods of the Lesser Path: creating vapor and fluid, applying fire and water, and mating the dragon and the tiger.

The production of vapor and fluid is the first step in the path to health. If these two carriers of generative energy are not produced in the body, no other alchemical interactions can occur.

Vapor and fluid mutually create each other. Yang vapor from the kidneys rises to the heart, which is also yang in nature. When the two yangs meet, yin is born. This yin is the fluid. The fluid descends and interacts with the yang of the kidneys to create vapor, which in turn rises to interact with the yang of the heart to produce fluid.

The production of vapor and fluid is patterned after the waxing and waning of the moon, and their natural ascent and descent in the body are patterned after the rise and fall of the yin and yang vapors in nature. The optimal time for gathering vapor and fluid is when the two substances are fresh and plentiful, that is, when they are initially produced.

The key to the Lesser Path lies in the mating of the dragon and the tiger.

The dragon and the tiger are, respectively, the yang and yin components of mundane generative energy. Therefore the dragon is sometimes called the yang dragon and the tiger is sometimes called the yin tiger. The yin tiger is the true water hidden in the vapor and is symbolized by the solid line in the trigram k'an (☵). The yang dragon is the true vapor hidden in the fluid and is symbolized by the broken line in the trigram li (☲). When the yin tiger and the yang dragon copulate, they are united and are transformed into the undifferentiated generative essence called the yellow sprouts. When internal heat is applied, the yellow sprouts (or primordial generative energy) will be transmuted into primordial vapor (primordial vital energy). The primordial vapor that is collected in the lower abdominal area is called the immortal fetus. This bundle of energy is stored in the lower tan-t'ien and can be used to replenish generative energy that has been lost.

The methods of the Lesser Path are discussed in chapters 7 through 10. Readers who want a detailed description of the process of producing, transforming, and unifying the yin and yang components of generative energy can refer to my *Harmonizing Yin and Yang*, a translation of the *Dragon-Tiger Classic*.

Hints for Reading This Section

- The interaction of the dragon and the tiger is the key to transforming mundane generative energy into primordial generative energy.
- Vapor and fluid are "carriers," respectively, of the yin and yang components of mundane generative energy. They are *not* equivalent to mundane generative energy.
- The yin tiger and the yang dragon *are* the components (or ingredients) of mundane generative energy. The yin tiger is hidden in the vapor and the yang dragon is hidden in

the fluid. In other words, *the vapor is the carrier of the yin tiger (yin generative energy) and the fluid is the carrier of the yang dragon (yang generative energy).*

- These are other names for the yin tiger: the one true water in the vapor, the fluid of pure yin, the one true water, and the silver in the lead. Don't mistake the fluid of pure yin for the fluid. The latter is the fluid of the heart, which is the carrier of the yang dragon.
- These are other names for the yang dragon: the one true vapor in the fluid, the vapor of pure yang, the one true vapor, and the mercury in the cinnabar. Don't mistake the vapor of pure yang for the vapor. The latter is the vapor of the kidneys, which is the carrier of the yin tiger.
- Make sure you understand that the interaction is between the yin tiger (the true water hidden in the vapor) and the yang dragon (the true vapor hidden in the fluid).
- You should also understand that the transformation of generative energy from its mundane to its primordial form is central to the Lesser Path. When mundane generative energy is purified into primordial generative energy, it can be used to revitalize the body. In other words, we are healthy when generative energy is purified and plentiful.
- The Lesser Path is concerned with strengthening the lower tan-t'ien. It ends when the yin and yang components of generative energy (tiger and dragon) are united to form the undifferentiated generative essence and when this essence is transmuted into primordial vapor (the immortal fetus).
- Again, don't get bogged down by the discussion of numerics.

The Arts of Longevity: The Methods and Benefits of the Middle Path

The Middle Path is concerned with cultivating longevity. Training in this path is involved with circulating the primordial vapor and transmuting it into primordial spirit energy. These are the methods of the Middle Path: directing the primordial generative essence to the head, initiating the Waterwheel (the Microcosmic and Macrocosmic Circulations), circulating the jade and golden elixirs and returning them to the elixir fields (tan-t'iens), and using the elixirs to refine the body.

The Middle Path begins with directing the primordial generative essence to the head. After the dragon and the tiger have copulated, the primordial generative essence will emerge from the area behind the navel. When this essence is directed to the top of the head, energy will shoot up the spine and enter the cranium. This process is called "extracting lead to replenish mercury," "returning the generative essence to the brain," or "ejecting the golden sparks from behind the navel."

The next stage in the Middle Path is to start the Waterwheel. The Waterwheel is the most important process in the Middle Path: it is *both* the Microcosmic and the Macrocosmic Circulations and it is the "vehicle" that moves energy in the body.

The movements that occur between the lower, middle, and upper tan-t'iens are collectively called "returning to the elixir fields (tan-t'ien)." When the contents of the lower tan-t'ien move to the middle tan-t'ien, generative energy (ching) is transmuted into vital energy (ch'i); when the contents of the middle tan-t'ien move to the lower tan-t'ien, vital energy is used to produce generative energy; when the contents of the middle tan-t'ien move to the upper tan-t'ien, vital energy is transmuted into spirit energy (shen); and when the contents of the upper tan-t'ien move to the middle tan-t'ien, spirit energy is used to produce vital energy.

Primordial vital energy is circulated as elixir. The effects of the circulation of the elixir are very visible: the body is rejuvenated and youthful vigor is recovered.

The methods of the Middle Path are discussed in chapters 11 through 14.

Hints for Reading This Section

• Make sure you understand the functions of the Water-wheel. The Small Waterwheel is used to cultivate health, the Great Waterwheel is used to cultivate longevity, and the Purple Waterwheel is used to cultivate immortality.

• The Waterwheel cannot be initiated until mundane generative energy has been transformed into primordial generative energy. Therefore, the Microcosmic and the Macro-cosmic Circulations cannot start until the body has accumulated enough primordial generative energy. Think of primordial generative energy as the fuel that drives the Waterwheel.

• The Waterwheel also cannot start until obstacles in its path have been cleared. In my experience, the momentum of the first "golden sparks" "flying up from behind the navel" is the key to opening the path for the Microcosmic and Macrocosmic Circulations. Many people describe the initial experience of "ejecting the golden sparks" as "something shooting up the spine."

• Although there are many types of "returns" of the elixir, they all follow this principle: the elixir begins its circulation at the place where it is produced; it is then moved to the target areas; finally it returns to the place of its origin.

• The elixir and the pill are two aspects of the same thing. In my experience, primordial vital energy that is stored is solid and is called the pill; primordial vital energy that is circulated is liquid and is called the elixir.

• Don't get bogged down by the numerics of the internal organs.

• The Middle Path is concerned with strengthening the middle tan-t'ien. It ends when primordial vital energy is transmuted into spirit energy.

The Arts of Immortality: The Methods and Benefits of the Great Path

The Great Path is concerned with cultivating immortality. Training in this path involves uniting the three primordial energies—generative, vital, and spirit—into the yang spirit (yang-shen) and liberating this spirit from the mundane body. These are the methods of the Great Path: moving the yang spirit to the primordial regions, meditating to "merge with the void," and releasing the yang spirit to merge with the cosmic energy of the Tao.

The most important practice in the Great Path is the meditation of "merging with the void." Other names that have been given to this form of meditation include "facing the wall" and "abiding in absolute stillness." While the Lesser and Middle Paths can be attained with a combination of calisthenics, internal martial arts, ch'i-kung exercises, and forms of meditation appropriate for those stages of training, the Great Path can be attained only by practicing the meditation of "merging with the void."

The methods of the Great Path are discussed in chapters 15 and 16.

Hints for Reading This Section

- Don't confuse internal observation discussed in the text with insight meditation (vipassana) or even Zen-style meditation. Internal observation as practiced in internal alchemy is used to liberate the spirit. In other words, it is practiced only when the practitioner is ready to shed the bodily shell and leave the mortal realm forever. Internal observation is also different from the kind of meditation that is used to still the mind in the early stages of cultivation. (For a modern and detailed discussion of the meditation of "merging with the void," refer to my *Cultivating the Energy of Life*, a translation of the *Hui-ming ching*.)
- The method of visualization described in chapter 16 disappeared from Taoist internal-alchemical texts soon after the *Chung-Lü ch'uan-tao chi* was written. As far as I know, the technique of visualization described in the text is no longer practiced among modern internal alchemists.

Obstacles and Landmarks of Spiritual Development

Finally, the text lists obstacles that can hinder a practitioner's spiritual progress and describes experiences that are considered landmarks in spiritual development. These topics are found in chapters 17 and 18.

Hint for Reading This Section

• Although chapter 17 appears toward the end of the book, it can be read out of sequence. I have found it to be a useful guide for cultivating the mind in daily living.

The *Chung-Lü ch'uan-tao chi* remains one of the most widely studied texts in the Taoist community today. It not only gives us valuable insights into the formative period of internal alchemy but is also one of the best beginner's guides to the Taoist art of health, longevity, and immortality. (The text is required reading for novices of the Complete Reality School, the Earlier Heaven Way, and the Green City sect.) While the strained parallels between the human body and the natural world are considered antiquated by modern practitioners, the programs of cultivating health, longevity, and immortality described in the text have not changed much since Lü Tung-pin first set down the teachings of Chungli Ch'uan more than a thousand years ago.

The Teachings of the Tao
As Transmitted by Chung and Lü

1

The True Immortals

Lü asked:
"What do we need to do if we want to be healthy and not ill, be young and not old, and live and not die?"

Chung said:
"We are conceived when our father and mother copulate and the two vapors [of creation] meet. The embryo is formed from generative fluid and blood. After the primal origin of things emerges, primal substance is created. Yang starts the process and yin completes it. As the vapor grows inside the womb, the fetus develops. After three hundred days, the form inside becomes round. When the luminous spirit enters the fetus, it will separate itself from the mother's body. After it emerges from the primal origin, its breath will rise and fall, and the yellow sprouts will begin to grow. In five thousand days, the vapor reaches its height. When the numerics add up to eighty-one, development is complete and we reach puberty. At the age of fifteen, half of yin is yang and we are as bright as the sun in the east. After puberty yang energy begins to wane. When the true vapor of life is spent, we will fall ill and die, for in our ignorance we have injured the light of the spirit.

"Evil deeds can also diminish our current life span as well as affect our disposition and longevity in the next lifetime. Thus, after we are born we die, and after we die we will be born again. When there is birth there will be death. Despite countless cycles of rebirth, we continue to be stubborn and ignorant. Thus, with each lifetime we sink lower and lower in the quagmire, until we are no longer born into human form. Once the wayward spirit enters a nonhuman shell, it will corrupt the original nature, and once the original spirit is corrupted, it will be difficult for it to become human again. Trapped in endless cycles of rebirth, it will never be liberated. If we are fortunate, we may meet an immortal who can help us lessen the karmic retribution and guide our spirit into a different shell. Then we will have a chance to become human again. If we manage to accumulate meritable deeds when we are in a nonhuman shell, we may eventually ascend to the higher realms of existence. Although we may be born crippled or destitute, we would have regained our human form. However, if we revert back to old habits and do unethical deeds, we will sink again into endless cycles of birth and death."

Lü said:

"People born in the central lands during times of peace do not have to worry about food and clothing. However, they are anxious that the years of their lives are passing too quickly. Everyone desires health and hates illness; everyone loves life and fears death. Today I have the privilege of meeting a great teacher. Therefore I would like to take this opportunity to ask you about matters concerning life and death, and hope that you will show me how to attain longevity and immortality."

Chung said:

"If people do not want to be reborn in the lower forms, they must overcome illness, aging, death, and suffering. They must stand with their heads against the sky and have their feet rooted in the earth. They must live their lives holding yin and embracing yang. In this way they will not become ghosts. If they cultivate themselves while they are in human form, they can become immortals. Later, as immortals, if they continue to cultivate, they will be able to ascend to the celestial realm."

Lü asked:

"When people die, they become ghosts. When they attain the Tao, they become immortals. Isn't immortality the highest goal of cultivation? Why do immortals 'need' to ascend to the celestial realm?"

Chung said:

"Becoming an immortal is not the ultimate goal of cultivation. A being who is entirely yin with no yang is a ghost. A being who is entirely yang with no yin is an immortal. Humans are half yin and half yang. Therefore they can become either ghosts or immortals. If we follow our desires and do not begin to cultivate [the Tao] when we are young, we will become ghosts when we die. On the other hand, if we are willing to cultivate, we will be able to transcend human existence, enter the sacred realm, shed the human shell, and become immortals. There are five classes of immortals and three paths of cultivation, and the level of immortality that you will attain will depend on the quality of your cultivation."

Lü asked:

"What are the three paths of cultivation and the five levels of immortality?"

Chung said:

"The three paths of cultivation are the Lesser Path, the Middle Path, and the Great Path. The five classes of immortals are ghost immortal, human immortal, earth immortal, spirit immortal, and celestial immortal. Ghost immortals do not leave the realm of ghosts; human immortals do not leave the realm of humanity; earth immortals do not leave the realm of earth; spirit immortals do not leave the realm of the spirit; and celestial immortals do not leave the celestial realm."

Lü asked:

"What are ghost immortals?"

Chung said:

"The ghost immortal is the lowest class of immortal. Ghost

immortals are beings who have attained immortality in the realm of the dead. Their spirit is dim and they have neither name nor title. Although they are not forced to be reborn, they are not able to enter the Peng-lai lands of immortality. They wander about in limbo between the realms of the living and the dead, and their existence comes to an end if they choose to be reborn into the human realm."

Lü asked:

"How do people become ghost immortals? What kinds of methods did they practice when they were alive?"

Chung said:

"People become ghost immortals when they try to cultivate but do not understand the Tao. Wanting to make fast progress, they take shortcuts in their training. As a result, their bodies are as brittle as dry wood and their minds are as dead as cold ashes. Hoping to keep the spirit within, they hold on to their intention. Thus, when they enter stillness, only the yin spirit is liberated. As a result, they become ghosts with no spirit; they cannot become immortals of pure yang. Because the yin spirit does not dissipate after they die, they are called ghost immortals. Although these beings are classed as immortals, they are really ghosts with no substance. Practitioners who claim to be Buddhist and who practice incorrectly the techniques of quiet sitting usually end up as this type of immortal."

Lü asked:

"What are human immortals?"

Chung said:

"The human immortal is the second lowest class of immortals. The human immortal is someone who cultivates but does not understand the Tao. Knowing only one method and practicing only one technique in that method, they work on one aspect of cultivation all their lives. As a result, the vapors of the five elements interact haphazardly and they have no control over the transformations inside their bodies. However, despite their mistakes, they have managed to cultivate a strong body that is immune to many diseases. This allows them to enjoy good health and live a long life in the human realm."

Lü asked:

"What kinds of methods did human immortals practice?"

Chung said:

"These people were taught the principles of the Great Tao when they started their cultivation. However, bad karma and monsters of the mind led their beginner's mind astray. As a result, they can get only small benefits from their cultivation. Although they follow the procedures of a method correctly, they are inflexible and cannot change with the seasons. Those who abstain from the five flavors do not know of the six vapors. Those who have tamed the seven emotions do not know of the ten abstinences. Those who practice swallowing the saliva denigrate those who practice breath control. Those who draw energy from a sexual partner consider those who practice singular methods stupid. Those who gather the vapors of the sky and the earth refuse to abstain from grains. Those who practice visualization and those who absorb the essences of the sun and the moon refuse to try the methods of massage and kneading. Those who attempt to slow their breath by sitting in silence do not understand what it means to practice naturally: they force their bodies into unnatural postures and do not understand the principle of noninterference.

"Then there are those who do not understand that absorbing the yin energy of females is not equivalent to drawing in the testicles during meditation. They also do not know that absorbing female energy by sucking on women's breasts is not equivalent to cultivating the elixir. I can't even begin to describe the kinds of things people do, hoping that one of the techniques will succeed in making them immortal. Although each technique works in a small way, it is not a complete path. Each technique is but one small aspect of one method within one path. If you practice only one technique, the best you can hope for is to live a healthy and long life. However, if these techniques are practiced incorrectly, they can be harmful. Instead of living a long life, the practitioner can become ill and may even die an early death. Such occurrences are not uncommon."

Lü asked:

"What are earth immortals?"

Chung said:

"Earth immortals stand halfway between the celestial and earthly realms. They have the potential to become spirit immortals, but because they do not have a complete understanding of the Tao, they can be content with only a moderate level of spiritual attainment. Their cultivation falls short of perfection, and the best they can do is to live forever in the human realm and not die."

Lü asked:

"How can we become an immortal of the earthly realm?"

Chung said:

"To become an earth immortal, you must first know how to control the ascent and descent of the vapors of heaven and earth. Model your cultivation after the numerics of the creation of the sky and the earth and follow the movement of the sun and the moon. Understand the yearly and monthly cycles of changes in your body. Monitor the hourly changes daily. First, be familiar with the dragon and the tiger, then subject them to the fires of k'an and li. Know the difference between pure water and muddy water, and learn how to distinguish between the vapors of the morning and the vapors of the evening. Second, gather that which is primordial and undifferentiated, keep track of the behavior of the two opposites, differentiate the three existences, separate the four directions, understand the five cycles, stabilize the six vapors, accumulate the seven treasures, balance the eight trigrams, and traverse the nine continents. Third, reverse the cycle of the five elements, channel the vapor of life to the fetus in the womb, and turn back the flow of procreative energy. Finally, circulate the energy in the three fields, forge the elixir with heat, and let it settle in the lower field. In this way the body will be preserved and you will live forever in the earthly realm."

Lü asked:

"What are spirit immortals?"

Chung said:

"Spirit immortals are earth immortals who have continued their cultivation in the earthly realm. They have connected all the parts of their body; they have used lead to replenish mercury; they can channel the refined generative energy to the top of the head; and they can transform the jade nectar into the elixir. Their bodily form has been transmuted into vapor; the five vapors have reverted back into the one primordial vapor; and the three yang essences have gathered at the top of the head. When their cultivation is complete, the mundane body is transformed into the subtle body. Their yin residues are purged and they are completely filled with pure yang. A body emerges from the subtle body as they shed their mundane substance and ascend to the immortal lands. Entering the realm of the sacred, they return to the three mountains and leave the dust of the world forever."

Lü asked:

"What are celestial immortals?"

Chung said:

"When earth immortals have refined themselves further through cultivation, they are able to shed their shell and become spirit immortals. When spirit immortals who dwell in the three islands have accumulated enough merits by teaching humanity about the Tao, and when their teachings have yielded fruits, they will be summoned by celestial decree to return to the celestial realm. Celestial immortals live in the celestial realm, fulfilling their duties as judges and officials within the celestial administration. They begin their duties as judges of the water realm. Then they are promoted to oversee the earth realm. Eventually they may become administrators of the sky [or celestial] realm. When they have accumulated enough merits in the lowest level of the celestial realm, they will be elevated to the next level, and so on until they have ascended through all thirty-six celestial realms. After going through the thirty-six celestial realms, they will work their way through the eighty-one levels of celestial yang, and after they have gone through the eighty-one levels of celestial yang, they will return to the three pure realms of the Natural Void."

Lü said:

"I don't want to be a ghost immortal and I don't dare to think about attaining celestial immortality. Can you tell me how to attain human, earth, and spirit immortality?"

Chung said:

"Human immortality is attainable using methods from the Lesser Path; earth immortality is attainable using methods from the Middle Path; and spirit immortality is attainable using methods from the Great Path. Although there are three paths, there is only one Way. If you follow these paths, you will find that the Tao is easy to understand. Having understood the Tao, you will find that immortality is only a step away."

Lü asked:

"Many practitioners past and present have tried to cultivate longevity and immortality and have failed. Why?"

Chung said:

"They failed because their methods are incorrect and because they do not understand the Tao fully. Some practitioners use information based on gossip and hearsay; some force themselves to learn what they do not understand; some invent their own techniques; yet others stray from the correct teachings. No wonder so many practitioners become ill and die early deaths! Then, there are those who claim that they can drive out monsters and those who confuse others with false teachings. Instead of listening to the true teachings of the Tao, they promote each other's incorrect methods. What a pity! Even if they practice diligently, they will achieve nothing."

2

The Great Tao

Lü asked:

"What is the Great Tao?"

Chung said:

"The Great Tao has no form and no name. It asks no questions and gives no answers. It is so large that it has no boundaries; it is so small that nothing can fit inside it. You cannot follow it even if you have heard about it; you cannot attain it even if you tried to practice it."

Lü said:

"Ever since the beginning of time, people have learned about the Tao, understood its principles, and attained it. After they attained the Tao, they left the dust of the world and went to the Peng-lai Islands. Then they ascended to the celestial realm, entered the realm of celestial yang, and eventually reached the Three Pure Realms. Honored teacher, why do you say that although people have heard of the Tao, they could not attain it, and although people have tried to practice its teachings, they could not reach it? Is it because the Tao wants to hide from us?"

Chung said:

"The Tao does not hide from us deliberately. People

couldn't attain the Tao because they did not trust its teachings, and those who trusted the teachings did not practice diligently. Some practiced it for one day and abandoned it the next day. Some remembered the principles in the beginning but forgot them later. Some started their training with enthusiasm but soon lost their interest. This is what I meant by the Tao being hard to attain even if you knew about it and tried to practice it."

Lü asked:

"Why is it so difficult to know about the Tao and practice its teachings?"

Chung said:

"It is because many people think that there are quick and easy ways to attain the Tao. They teach one another, not knowing that all their lives they have been practicing incorrectly. With time these erroneous methods became established, and the real teachings of the Tao are forgotten.

"Abstaining from meat, abstaining from grains, absorbing the vapors of fog and dew, swallowing saliva, living in isolation, meditating in ch'an (zen) stillness, maintaining silence, visualizing the deities, gathering yin energy, regulating breath, being celibate, stopping thinking, abstaining from physical labor, opening the cavity on top of the head, drawing in the testicles, studying the scriptures, tempering the body, slowing the breath, massaging, circulating the breath, gathering generative energy from a partner, helping the poor, cultivating the self, doing charitable works, living in the mountains, taming the mind, facing the wall, chanting the scriptures, absorbing the essences of the sun and the moon, and inhaling the vapors of the sky and the earth—these are just some of the techniques that people think will help them create the cinnabar pill of immortality. Hoping to be liberated from mundane existence, they force the body into unnatural postures and end up injuring themselves. They try to conserve generative energy by stopping the leakage of seminal fluid but do not know that these methods can make them immune only to common diseases. They think that if they can breathe like an infant and if they can stop thinking, they can cultivate the mind. They focus on retaining the breath within and try to build the fortress by reversing the flow of the Yellow River, not knowing that these techniques are only minor ways of lengthening the life span. As for sitting like a withered tree and making the mind as still as cold ashes—these are but minor techniques of focusing the spirit.

"Many practitioners past and present are ignorant of the correct methods of cultivation. How can their bodies be transmuted if they are stuck in the belief that they can cultivate the medicine by swallowing saliva? How can they hold on to the elixir if they are convinced that they can realize the pill by gathering the breath? How can the true copulation take place if they think that the liver is the dragon and the lungs are the tiger? How can they replenish the life force if they equate k'an with lead and li with mercury? They think that the yellow sprouts will grow if they apply fire and water in the four seasons. They also think that they will realize the great medicine if they hold on to the intention. Ignorant of the yearly and monthly cycles of changes, they do the wrong things at the wrong time. They do not know how to use the five elements to build the foundation and they have only vague ideas about the workings of the three existences. Like inexperienced gardeners rummaging through branches and leaves, they confuse fellow practitioners and mislead future generations of students.

"When the teachings are distorted, people will be distanced from the Tao. As a result, false methods will proliferate. The popular ones will be practiced widely and will eventually be accepted as truth. In my opinion the false teachers are to blame. They have taken information gathered through hearsay and gossip and have taught it to generations of unknowing students. In doing so, their actions have condemned their followers to suffering in the realm of the dead. This is very frightening indeed. The sages have always wanted to reveal the teachings of the Tao, but people throw away the opportunities to learn. In refusing to believe in the workings of heaven and in valuing their wealth more than their life, they have doomed themselves to the realm of ghosts."

Lü asked:

"Now that I've heard about the minor techniques and the misleading ways, can you tell me about the Great Tao?"

Chung said:

"There is nothing to ask about the Tao. There is also nothing that it cannot answer. When the Great Simplicity of the true origin divided, the Tao gave birth to the One. The One gave birth to the Two, and the Two gave birth to the Three. The One is structure, the Two is function, and the Three is transformation. Structure and form are nothing but yin and yang, and transformation is the result of yin and yang copulating. There are three realms—upper, middle, and lower. They are sky, earth, and humanity, respectively. Each realm has a piece of the Tao in it. The Tao gave birth to the yin and yang vapors and the two vapors gave birth to the three realms. The three realms gave birth to the five elements and the five elements gave birth to all the myriad things. Of all creation, only humans have the potential to attain the Tao. This is because humans can penetrate the principles of the Tao and understand themselves. By penetrating the principles and understanding themselves, they can preserve their life. By preserving their life and cultivating longevity, they can merge with the Tao. And by merging with the Tao, they can be as firm as the sky and the earth and can last forever."

Lü said:

"Sky and earth can last for a long time. When people live a hundred years, it is considered a long life. Even people who live to be seventy are rare. If the Tao is present in the sky and the earth, then why is it so difficult to reach?"

Chung said:

"The Tao is never far from humanity. It is humanity that has moved away from the Tao. People nowadays are distant from the Tao because they do not know the method of cultivating life. If you do not know the method of cultivating life, then you will not be able to do the right thing at the right time, and if you are ignorant of the schedule of the cyclical changes, you will not be able to penetrate the secret workings of heaven and earth."

3

Heaven and Earth

Lü asked:

"May I learn about the workings of heaven and earth?"

Chung said:

"The workings of heaven and earth are the ways in which the Great Tao is manifested in the universe. Upward and downward, it moves without ceasing. This is why heaven and earth have a secure foundation and can last for a long time. The secrets of their workings are not normally revealed to humankind."

Lü asked:

"How is the Tao manifested in heaven and earth? How can we understand the secrets of its movement? How can we initiate it? And when it is in motion, how can we recognize its effects?"

Chung said:

"The Great Tao takes on a form when it is manifested in heaven and earth. With form, the numerics emerged. The way of ch'ien is manifested in heaven and the numeric of its structure is one. That which is light and pure rises because its function is yang in nature. The way of k'un is manifested in earth and the numeric of its structure is two. That which is heavy and muddy sinks because its function is yin in nature. When yang rises and yin sinks, they will interact with each other. This is the way of ch'ien and k'un, and it is the way the Tao works. There is a time to get things started and there is a time to collect the results."

Lü asked:

"The way of ch'ien is manifested in heaven and it follows the function of yang. Since yang governs ascent, how can it sink and interact with earth? The way of k'un is manifested in earth and it follows the function of yin. Since yin governs descent, how can it rise and interact with heaven? If heaven and earth do not interact, how can yin and yang be united? If yin and yang are not united, how can ch'ien and k'un perform their functions? If ch'ien and k'un do not perform their functions, how can things get started and be completed?"

Chung said:

"In the way of heaven, ch'ien is structure, yang is function, and its vapor accumulates at the top. In the way of earth, k'un is structure, yin is function, and its water accumulates at the bottom.

"When heaven follows the principles of the Tao, ch'ien (heaven ☰) will seek out k'un (earth ☷). In the first interaction, the eldest male emerges, and it is called chen (thunder ☳). In the next interaction, the middle male emerges, and it is called k'an (water ☵). In the third interaction, the youngest male emerges, and it is called ken (mountain ☶). When heaven approaches earth, ch'ien will interact with k'un and will give birth to the three yangs.

"When earth follows the principles of the Tao, k'un will seek out ch'ien. In the first interaction, the eldest female emerges, and it is called sun (wind ☴). In the next interaction, the middle female emerges, and it is called li (fire ☲). In the third interaction, the youngest female emerges, and it is called tui (lake ☱). When earth approaches heaven, k'un will interact with ch'ien and give birth to the three yins.

"When the three yangs interact with the three yins, the ten

thousand myriad things are born. When the three yins interact with the three yangs, the ten thousand myriad things are nourished. The interaction of heaven and earth is founded on the natural attraction between yin and yang, and this attraction is part of the natural way of the Tao.

"Ch'ien and k'un interact to give birth to the six vapors. The six vapors interact to create the five elements. The five elements interact to create and nourish the ten thousand things. Ch'ien finishes its course of descent when the three interactions are completed. Thereafter yang rises again. Consequently the yin that is hidden in the yang also rises and returns to heaven. K'un finishes its course of ascent when the three interactions are completed. Thereafter yin sinks again. Consequently the yang that is hidden in the yin also sinks and returns to earth.

"When the yin in the yang cannot be exhausted by use, it is the true yin. When the true yin reaches heaven, it will meet yang and be energized. Since yin descends from heaven, how can we say that there is no yang within the yin? Yang is hidden in yin. When the yang in the yin does not dissipate, it is the true yang. When the true yang reaches earth, it will meet yin and be renewed. Since yang rises from earth, how can we say that there is no yin within the yang? Yin is hidden within yang. Always returning to earth, this yin never dissipates. Yang is hidden within yin. Always returning to heaven, this yang never extinguishes. This cycle of ascent and descent continues forever because the interaction of yin and yang is governed by the principles of the Tao. It is because of this that heaven and earth have a secure foundation and can last for a long time."

Lü said:

"Because heaven and earth follow the principles of the Tao, they can last for a long time. We see this clearly in the workings of the universe. What about humankind? How can the workings of the Tao be realized in intelligent people who cultivate clarity and stillness and live according to the principles of the Tao? I am told that if they follow the Lesser Path of cultivation, they can enjoy a happy and long life; if they follow the Middle Path of cultivation, they can attain longevity and not die; and if they follow the Great Path of cultivation, they can transcend their mundane nature and become immortals. How can we embody the Tao and apply its principles? How can we follow the workings of heaven so that we too can be firm and stable and last forever?"

Chung said:

"The Great Tao originally has no form. It is only because of the existence of 'the other' that it has acquired a form. The Great Tao has no name. It is only because 'the other' is named that it has acquired a name. When the Tao is manifested in heaven and earth, it is the way of ch'ien and k'un. When it is manifested in the sun and the moon, it is the way of yin and yang. When it is manifested in human society, it is the way of ruler and minister. In the bedchamber it is the way of husband and wife; in the social community it is the way of elders and children; in the circle of acquaintances it is the way of friends; and in the family it is the way of father and son. Everything follows the principles of the Tao in its own way.

"When our father and mother copulate, the yang of the father moves first. Yin follows later. As the true vapor connects with the true water, the fire of the heart and the water of the kidneys will interact. In this way the essence of procreative energy (ching) is refined. When the essence of the procreative energy emerges and encounters the yin of the female, the waters are swirled in the areas of nonactivity. When it encounters the yang of the female, blood is stirred and collected in the womb. The fetus contains the essence of the procreative blood of the female. It also embodies the true vapor, because in copulation the vapor is directed into the womb of the female. With time the true vapor will be transformed into a human being. This process is patterned after the workings of heaven and earth. It is also modeled after the way in which ch'ien and k'un are attracted to each other and the way in which they give birth to the three yins and the three yangs.

"The true vapor is yang and the true water is yin. The yang is hidden in the water and the yin is hidden in the vapor. Vapor governs ascending movement, and inside the vapor is the true water. Water governs descending movement, and inside the water is the true vapor. Thus the true water is the true yin and the true vapor is the true yang. The true yang descends, following the path of the water. Behaving like ch'ien, it moves to meet k'un, creating chen (thunder) when it is on top, k'an (water) when it is in the middle, and ken (mountain) when it is at the bottom. In the human body, movement spreads upward and downward from the middle. Thus chen is the liver, k'an is the kidneys, and ken is the bladder. The true yin ascends, following the path of the vapor. Behaving like k'un, it moves to meet ch'ien, creating sun (wind) when it is at the bottom, li (fire) when it is in the middle, and tui (lake) when it is at the top. In the human body, movement spreads upward and downward from the middle. Thus sun is the gall bladder, li is the heart, and tui is the lungs. When its form is developed and the numerics are complete, the fetus will leave the mother's body.

"After birth the primordial yang is stored in the kidneys. The primordial vapor gives birth to the true vapor, and the true vapor moves toward the heart. The true vapor gives birth to the true water and then returns to the origin. From there it circulates up and down through the body without stopping. If the vapor does not leak out of the body, you will live a long life. If you know the rhythm of its movement and know how to replenish it in the appropriate way, you will never grow old. If you work hard in your cultivation, the yin will dissipate, the yang will be pure, and you will be able to transcend mortality and enter the sacred. These are the principles of the hidden workings of heaven. They have not been transmitted past or present.

"If you are sincere and are without doubts, if you view

fame and fortune as chains, if you consider passion and desire as thieves, if you abhor illness and death, if you don't want to lose your human form and let your spirit enter the shell of an animal, and if you have the inclination to cultivate clarity and stillness, then you should seek to return to the origin and not let your primordial yang dissipate. Let the true vapor spread until there is no yin left in your spirit. When yang is strong, the soul will be filled with vapor. The cycle of ascent and descent parallels the workings of heaven and earth, and the cycle of the flow and ebb of yin and yang is similar to the changes manifested in the course of the sun and the moon."

4

Sun and Moon

Lü asked:

"Now that I have a crude understanding of the workings of heaven and earth, can you tell me how to apply the laws of the sun and the moon to our body?"

Chung said:

"The Great Tao has no form, but it created heaven and earth. The Great Tao has no name but it keeps the sun and the moon in their course. The sun and the moon are the essences of the Great Yang and the Great Yin. They reveal to us the limits of the interaction of heaven and earth and are the force behind the creation and completion of the ten thousand things. Rising and setting along the east-west axis, they differentiate day and night. Moving between south and north, they anchor the seasons. Night is followed by day and cold is followed by warmth—the cycle never stops. The spirit emerges within the soul and the soul emerges within the spirit, their waxing and waning following a course that is part of the numerics of ch'ien and k'un. Their movements have a limit and do not stray from the seasonal changes in heaven and earth."

Lü asked:

"What is meant by day and night being delineated by the rising and setting along the east-west axis?"

Chung said:

"In the beginning, when the primordial whole split open and divided itself, the Subtle Yellow anchored the directions. Heaven and earth took on the shape of an egg. Round like a sphere, the cosmos encloses the six vapors within. Moving across the sky, the sun and the moon rise and set along the east-west axis like an ever turning wheel. The time between the sun's rising in the east and its setting in the west is called day. The time between the sun's setting in the west and its rising in the east is called night. This is what is meant by day and night being delineated by the rising and setting of the sun.

"The moon is different from the sun. The moon receives its soul from the west and its spirit from the east. Its light shines at night and its spirit is hidden during the day. As it moves through the days of the month, it is sometimes visible and sometimes not. When the moon moves from west to east, the spirit emerges in the soul. When the new moon first appears, it is shaped like a bow, and in the early part of the night it illuminates the west. In the next phase the spirit occupies half of the soul. The moon is now in its first quarter. In the early part of the night it illuminates the south. In the next phase the soul is completely filled with the spirit, and the moon is as bright as the sun. In the early part of the night it illuminates the east. In the next phase the soul emerges in the spirit, and the moon is shaped like an incomplete mirror. In the early part of the night the spirit is hidden in the west. In the next phase the soul occupies half of the spirit. The moon is now in its last quarter. In the early part of the night it illuminates the south. In the next phase the spirit is completely filled with the soul. Now it is behind the sun. In the early part of the night the spirit is hidden in the east. This is what is meant by day and night being delineated by the waxing and waning of the moon."

Lü asked:

"What is meant by cold and warmth being anchored by movement along the north-south axis?"

Chung said:

"At the winter solstice the sun rises sometime in the first fifty minutes after the hour of chen [between 7:00 and 7:50 A.M.] and sets sometime in the last fifty minutes before the hour of shen [between 4:10 and 5:00 P.M.]. Its path follows a definite course, moving progressively from south to north. The sun continues to move north until the summer solstice. At the summer solstice the sun rises sometime in the last fifty minutes before the hour of yin [between 4:10 and 5:00 A.M.] and sets sometime in the last fifty minutes after the hour of hsü [between 7:00 and 7:50 P.M.]. Its path follows a definite course, moving progressively from north to south. The sun continues to move south until the winter solstice. When the sun moves from south to north between the winter and summer solstices, cold changes to warmth. When it moves from north to south between the summer and winter solstices, warmth changes to cold. The summer sun is the night of winter and the winter sun is the night of summer. After the winter solstice the moon, like the summer sun, rises northerly and then moves south. After the summer solstice the moon, like the winter sun, rises southerly and then moves north."

Lü asked:

"The rise and fall of yin and yang in heaven and earth parallel the ascent and descent of vapor in the human body. Do the principles that govern the rising, the setting, and the movement of the sun and the moon also apply to the human body?"

Chung said:

"The workings of heaven and earth are found in the rise and fall of yin and yang. In their ascent and descent, the two opposites in the t'ai-chi mutually create and nourish each other. This process never stops. Therefore heaven and earth can last as long as the Tao.

"If you live in accordance with the principles of heaven

45

and earth, you will enjoy a long life and not die. However, if you can model yourself after the movements of the sun and the moon, if you can receive the spirit of the sun in the moon and transform yang into yin, and if you can extinguish the yin completely, the yang within you will be pure. When the essence of the moon is full and clear, the yin spirit will disappear. When yin disappears, you will be like the bright sun illuminating the earth. However, if in addition you can use the vapor to complete the spirit, you will be able to shed your bodily shell and become an immortal. This is what is meant by 'cultivating the body of pure yang.'"

Lü asked:

"For the followers of the Tao who cultivate the true essence, which procedure should be practiced first—applying the principles of the rise and fall of yin and yang in heaven and earth, or initiating the interaction of the essences in accordance with the movement of the sun and the moon?"

Chung said:

"The method of following the workings of heaven should be applied first. Use the principles of the rise and fall of yin and yang to unite the true water and the true fire. Refine them into the great medicine and let the medicine guard the elixir field (tan-t'ien). In this way you will be able to escape suffering and death and live as long as heaven and earth. Should you decide to continue your cultivation after you have attained longevity in this realm, then you should apply the principles of the interaction of the sun and the moon to your body. Use yang to refine yin and do not let yin emerge. Use the vapor to nourish the spirit so that the spirit will not dissipate. In this way the five vapors will move toward the primordial regions, the three flowers will gather at the top of the head, and you will be able to leave the mundane world and return to the three islands."

Lü said:

"These methods are profound and wonderful. It's a pity that nobody wants to hear about them."

Chung said:

"In the cycle of the rise and fall of yin and yang, heaven and earth interact once every year. In the movement of the sun and the moon, their essences interact once every month. In the human body, however, vapor and liquid interact once every cycle of day and night."

5

The Four Periods of Time

Lü asked:

"May I hear about the interaction of the sun and the moon and the periods of time in the year, month, and day?"

Chung said:

"There are four periods of time. Each person has a life span of one hundred years. Between the first and the thirtieth year is the period of youth and strength. Between the thirtieth and the sixtieth year is the period of growth and maturity. Between the sixtieth and the ninetieth year is the period of aging. Between the ninetieth and the one hundredth or one hundred twentieth year is the period of decay. This is the period of time in the body; it is the first of the four periods of time.

"There are twelve two-hour partitions in each day. Five days constitute one week. Three weeks make up one fifteen-day cycle. Three fifteen-day cycles make up one minor change in the weather, and two minor changes in the weather make up one season [or one major change in the weather]. The seasons are spring, summer, autumn, and winter. In spring half of yin is yang. Thus in spring the weather changes from cold to warm. In summer all of yang is yang. Thus in summer the weather changes from warm to hot. In autumn half of yang is yin. Thus in autumn the weather changes from hot to cool. In winter all of yin is yin. Thus in winter the weather changes from cool to cold. This is the period of time in the year; it is the second of the four periods of time.

"There are thirty days and three hundred sixty two-hour partitions in one lunar month. From the new moon to the first quarter moon, half of yin is yang. From the first quarter to the full moon, all of yang is yang. From the full moon to the last quarter, half of yang is yin. From the last quarter to no moon, all of yin is yin. This is the period of time in the sun and the moon; it is the third of the four periods of time.

"There are sixty minutes in an hour. Eight hours and twenty minutes make up one temporal segment. One and a half temporal segments map onto one trigram [k'ua]. The trigrams anchor the eight directions. Looking at the four cardinal directions, from tzu (north) to mao (east), half of yin is yang. At this time lesser yang is born within the great yin. From mao (east) to wu (south), all of yang is yang. At this time pure yang (or great yang) emerges from the lesser yang. From wu (south) to yu (west), half of yang is yin. At this time lesser yin arises from the great yang. From yu (west) to tzu (north), all of yin is yin. At this time pure yin (great yin) emerges from the lesser yin. This is the period of time in the day; it is the fourth of the four periods of time.

"The period of time in the body is the most difficult to hold on to; it is also the easiest to lose. The periods of time in the year and the month come slowly but pass quickly. Swift as lightning and short-lived as the spark of fire from flint is the period of time in the days and the hours. The days accumulate to become months and the months accumulate to become years. With each passing year we are left with a little less time in our lives. The years pass even more quickly for people who desire fame and fortune and for those who cannot subdue their wayward minds. Attached to children and grandchildren, they are flooded by the rise and fall of feelings and emotions. Only those who return to the Tao with all their heart can battle the onset of old age and decay. Spring snow and autumn flowers do not last long, and light from the setting sun and the sickle moon is weak. For those who follow the Tao, the period of time in the body is the most valuable.

"Surrounded by beauty, sensual pleasures, and a hundred perfume fragrances, people do not realize that the floodwaters are weakening the foundations of their houses. Delighting in the soft breeze, they talk long into the night and drink with their friends through the winter days. They pursue pleasure, wasting their time on things that do not last. If only they could awaken and turn their hearts back to the Tao! Even if you are suffering from illness or are in pain, it is not too late to return to the Tao. No one wants to go down with a sinking boat. Repair the leaks in your house and work hard to cultivate yourself. My advice to those who want to cultivate the Tao is this: don't idle away the years and the hours.

"Before the rooster crows, you are out of the house. When the town crier announces the coming of evening, you complain that it is too early to return home. Greed prevents you from stopping and resting. Desire makes you worry that you don't have enough. Your house may be filled with gold, but you are weak and helpless when you are ill. Seeing your children and grandchildren at your bedside, you worry that no one will look after them when you die. People do not understand that day and night follow each other and that time does not wait. Therefore, those who cultivate the Tao must value each day."

Lü asked:

"The periods of time in the body, the year, the sun and moon, and the day are all manifestations of the passage of time. Why do you, honored teacher, consider the period of time in the body to be the most precious and the period of time in the day to be the most valuable?"

Chung said:

"For those who cultivate the Tao, the most important time of their life is youth, because the roots of the origin are strong and stable in young people. Young practitioners can attain the fruits of cultivation easily and can achieve wondrous results in a thousand days. The years of growth and maturity are also valuable to those who cultivate the Tao. However, people who begin their cultivation in middle age must first replenish the energy that they have lost. Then they should work to increase what they have gathered. Initially they will be able to reverse aging and recover their youth. Later they may be able to transcend the mundane and enter the sacred. Even if you do not understand the need to cultivate in your youth, even if you don't know how to conserve your life force in your middle years, even if it is only through suffering that you have come to recognize the value of clarity and stillness, and even if you start to understand the intangible and invisible only after you have been ill, you can still begin to cultivate [the Tao] in your old age. Those who start their cultivation in their later years must first try to save the energy that is left in them. Next they should replenish energy that was lost. In this way they can gradually enter the Lesser Path. Then, as they accumulate merit by doing charitable deeds, they will be able to enter the Middle Path. Finally, continuing their cultivation in the Middle Path, they will be able to reverse aging and recover their youth. However, even though they can preserve their body in the earthly realm, their five vapors will not be able to flow toward the primordial regions and the three flowers will not gather on top of their heads. Because they started their cultivation late, it is not possible for them to become immortals. Therefore the period of time in the body is the most precious."

Lü asked:

"Now I understand why the period of time in the body is the most precious. Can you tell me why the period of time in the day is so valuable?"

Chung said:

"One day in the life of humans is equivalent to one month in the life of the sun and the moon and one year in the life of the sky and the earth. The Great Tao gave birth to the sky and the earth, and sky and earth are divided into an upper and a lower region. The two regions are separated by eighty-four thousand measures. After the winter solstice, the vapor of yang in the earth rises. A change in the weather occurs every fifteen days. This is because in every fifteen days the yang vapor ascends seven thousand measures. In one hundred eighty days, the rising yang vapor reaches the sky, and the Great Ultimate (t'ai-chi) will give birth to the great yin. After summer solstice yin descends from the sky. A change in the weather occurs every fifteen days. This is because, again, in every fifteen days the yin vapor descends seven thousand measures. In one hundred eighty days, the descending yin vapor reaches the earth and the Great Ultimate will give birth to yang. When one phase ends, the other begins. This cycle continues forever, following the principles of the Tao.

"The sun and the moon travel in their course across the sky without fail. When the sun and the moon were created, each was set to traverse eight hundred forty measures in one phase of their movement. After the birth of the moon [new moon], the nine emerges in the six. In the twelve two-hour partitions of the day, the spirit within the soul advances seventy measures. Every fifteen days, or one hundred eighty two-hour segments, the spirit within the soul advances eight hundred forty measures. After the full moon, the six emerges in the nine. In the twelve two-hour partitions of the day, the soul in the spirit advances seventy measures. Every fifteen days, or one hundred eighty two-hour segments, the soul in the spirit advances eight hundred forty measures. When one phase ends, the other begins. This cycle continues forever, following the principles of the Tao.

"It is in this way that the foundation of the Tao is built and the ten thousand things are nourished. Of all living things, humanity has the spark of the spirit and is the most intelligent. In the human body the heart and the kidneys are separated by eight and four-tenths [Chinese] inches. [One Chinese 'foot' equals approximately fourteen English inches.] The ascent and descent of yin and yang follow the behavior of the sky and the earth. Fluid emerges from vapor and vapor emerges from fluid. Fluid and vapor mutually give birth to each other, following the behavior of the sun and the moon. In the sky and the earth, ch'ien and k'un mutually seek out each other. In accordance with the rise and the fall of yin and yang, they copulate once a year, following the principles of the Tao. Each year is followed by another year. The birth of the spirit and the soul parallels the course of the sun and the moon. Their essences flow and ebb and they copulate once a month in accordance with the principles of the Tao. Each month is followed by another month. In humans the moment of convergence occurs once every day and night [twenty-four hours]. If you do not know the time of the convergence, if you are unfamiliar with the method of gathering, if you do not know how to replenish that which was lost, if you do not gather it when it is plentiful, if during the height of yin you do not cultivate the yang, if during the height of yang you do not refine the yin, if you do not know that you are losing your life force every month, and if you do not practice every day, then with each passing year you will have lost one year of your life, and with each passing day you will have lost one day of your life. If you are unwilling to cultivate [the Tao], then you are no different from those who sleep in wet clothes in a draughty room and those who endure the summer heat and brave winter storms: you all choose to be ill. If you idle your time away, then you are no different from those who are waiting to die."

Lü said:

"Those who cultivate the Tao must not idle away their time. As the years pass, the body will become weaker and weaker and you will get closer and closer to death. However, if you practice the wrong method, you won't get any results either: the yin and yang in your body will not copulate on schedule and the timing of the daily and monthly interactions will be off."

Chung said:

"You must apply the schedule of the year in the body, apply the schedule of the month in the year, and apply the schedule of the hour in the day. This is because the vapors of the five viscera flow and ebb in specific times in the month and rise and fall during specific times of the day. Every hour the vapors move five degrees, and every six temporal segments they complete one circuit of circulation. The process is the same for metal, wood, water, fire, and earth. East, west, south, north, and center all have their numerics of birth and completion.

"If the schedules are followed correctly, then the procreative energy can be refined and transmuted into true vapor, the true vapor can be refined and united with the yang spirit, and the spirit can be refined and merged with the Great Tao."

6

The Five Elements

Lü said:

"The vapors of the five viscera are metal, wood, water, fire, and earth; the positions of the five elements are east, west, south, north, and center, respectively. How do they create and complete each other? Do they interact at specific times? When should they be gathered? I'd like to hear what you have to say about these things."

Chung said:

"From the Great Tao comes the sky and the earth. When sky and earth divided, the five emperors emerged. The green emperor of the east is the ruler of spring. During this season yang rises within yin and gives birth to the ten thousand things. The red emperor of the south is the ruler of summer. During this season yang rises within yang and makes the ten thousand things grow. The white emperor of the west is the ruler of autumn. During this season yin rises within yang and directs all things to complete their course of development. The black emperor of the north is the ruler of winter. During this season yin rises within yin and makes all things decay and die. In the ninety days of a season, eighteen days are set aside in each season [for the yellow emperor]. In spring the yellow emperor in the center assists the green emperor to give birth to all things. In summer he encourages the red emperor to help things grow. In autumn he helps the white emperor to let things mature. In winter he supports the black emperor to ensure that all things are at rest. The five emperors each rule seventy-two days. Together they rule the three hundred sixty days of the year; together they help the sky and the earth follow the principles of the Tao.

"The sons of the green emperor are chia and i, and chia and i belong to the wood element in the east. The sons of the red emperor are ping and ting, and ping and ting belong to the fire element in the south. The sons of the yellow emperor are wu and chi, and wu and chi belong to the earth element in the center. The sons of the white emperor are keng and hsin, and keng and hsin belong to the metal element in the west. The sons of the black emperor are jen and kuei, and jen and kuei belong to the water element in the north. [Chia, i, ping, ting, wu, chi, keng, hsin, jen, kuei are the Ten Celestial Stems.] When the emperors interact with the seasons, the directions emerge. Wood is manifested as the green dragon, fire as the red raven, earth as the yellow worm, metal as the white tiger, and water as the black tortoise. In their interaction with the seasons, the five emperors create the ten thousand myriad things.

"When i is combined with keng, elm trees will bloom in spring. Green will take on a white tint, embodying the colors of metal and wood. When hsin is combined with ping, dates will be plentiful in autumn. White will take on a red tint, embodying the colors of metal and fire. When chi is combined with chia, melons will ripen in late summer and early autumn. Green will take on a yellow tint, embodying the colors of earth and wood. When ting is combined with jen, mushrooms will sprout in summer. Red will take on a black tint, embodying the colors of water and fire. When kuei is combined with wu, there will be nutmeg oranges in winter. Black will take on a yellow tint, embodying the colors of water and earth. It is in this way that all things are created, nourished, and grouped into their natural categories. It is said that when the five emperors interact with the seasons, there is no limit to the kinds of things that they can create."

Lü asked:

"So, this is how the five elements interact with the seasons. May I ask how do they interact inside us?"

Chung said:

"The human head is round and the legs are angular. Therefore humans take on the shape of the sky and the earth. When yin descends, yang rises. The movement of the vapors of yin and yang within us parallels the workings of the sky and the earth. The kidneys are water, the heart is fire, the liver is wood, the lungs are metal, and the spleen is earth. When the five elements give birth to each other, water creates wood, wood creates fire, fire creates earth, earth creates metal, and metal creates water. That which gives birth is called the mother and that which is born is called the son. When the five elements tame each other, water tames fire, fire tames metal, metal tames wood, wood tames earth, and earth tames water. That which tames is called the husband and that which is tamed is called the wife.

"In the mother-son relationship, the vapor of the kidneys strengthens the vapor of the liver, the vapor of the liver strengthens the vapor of the heart, the vapor of the heart strengthens the vapor of the spleen, the vapor of the spleen strengthens the vapor of the lungs, and the vapor of the lungs strengthens the vapor of the kidneys. In the husband-wife relationship, the vapor of the kidneys tames the vapor of the heart, the vapor of the heart tames the vapor of the lungs, the vapor of the lungs tames the vapor of the liver, the vapor of the liver tames the vapor of the spleen, and the vapor of the spleen tames the vapor of the kidneys. The kidneys are the husband of the heart, the mother of the liver, the wife of the spleen, and the son of the lungs. The liver is the husband of the spleen, the mother of the heart, the wife of the lungs, and the son of the kidneys. The heart is the husband of the lungs, the mother of the spleen, the wife of the kidneys, and the son of the liver. The lungs are the husband of the liver, the mother of the kidneys, the wife of the heart, and the son of the spleen. The spleen is the husband of the kidneys, the mother of the lungs, the wife of the liver, and the son of the heart.

"Internally the heart is manifested in the meridians; externally it is manifested as complexion. Its opening is in the tongue. It tames the lungs and is tamed by the kidneys. In this respect it follows the principles of the husband-wife relationship. When the heart encounters the liver, it is strengthened. When it encounters the spleen, its strength is diminished. In this respect it follows the principle of the mother-son relationship.

"Internally the kidneys are manifested in the bones; externally they are manifested as hairs. Their openings are in the ears. They tame the heart and are tamed by the spleen. In this respect they follow the principles of the husband-wife relationship. When the kidneys encounter the lungs, they are strengthened. When they encounter the liver, their strength is diminished. In this respect they follow the principle of the mother-son relationship.

"Internally the liver is manifested in the tendons; externally it is manifested as the finger- and toenails. Its openings are in the eyes. It tames the spleen and is tamed by the lungs. In this respect it follows the principles of the husband-wife relationship. When the liver encounters the kidneys, it is strengthened. When it encounters the heart, its strength is diminished. In this respect it follows the principle of the mother-son relationship.

"Internally the lungs are manifested as the hollow organs; externally they are manifested as pores on the skin. Their openings are the nostrils. They tame the liver and are tamed by the heart. In this respect they follow the principles of the husband-wife relationship. When the lungs encounter the spleen, they are strengthened. When they encounter the kidneys, their strength is diminished. In this respect they follow the mother-son relationship.

"Internally the spleen is manifested as the viscera. It nourishes the heart, kidneys, lungs, and liver. Externally it is manifested as the skin. Its opening is the mouth, and during inhalation and exhalation, it tames the kidneys and is tamed by the liver. In this respect it follows the principles of the husband-wife relationship. When the spleen encounters the heart, it is strengthened. When it encounters the lungs, its strength is diminished. In this respect it follows the principle of the mother-son relationship. These are the ways in which the five elements nourish and tame each other inside the body. The ways in which vapor is transferred, strengthened, and weakened are all embodied in the relationships among the husband, wife, mother, and son."

Lü said:

"The heart belongs to the element fire. How can we make the fire sink? The kidneys belong to the element water. How can we make the water rise? The spleen belongs to the element earth. Since earth is in the middle, the spleen will be strengthened when it receives the sinking fire. However, doesn't this diminish the strength of the water below it? The lungs belong to the element metal. Since metal is on top, the lungs will be damaged when they encounter the fire below. How can they create water? The elements that can nourish each other are far away, thus making it difficult to bring them together. On the other hand, the elements that tame each other are near, thus making it difficult to pull them apart. If this is true, the five elements will mutually damage each other. How can we solve this problem?"

Chung said:

"The undifferentiated vapor directs the five elements to return to the origin. The primordial yang rises to give birth to the true water. The true water transmutes to give birth to the true vapor. The true vapor transmutes to give birth to the yang spirit.

"Right from the start, when the positions of the five elements are established, the husband-wife relationship emerges. The kidneys are water. In water is metal, and metal naturally gives birth to water. Therefore, when you begin your cultivation, you must recognize the metal within the water. Water is naturally tamed by earth. Therefore, when you gather the medicine, you must get water to obey earth. The dragon is the manifestation of the spirit of the liver and the tiger is the manifestation of the spirit of the lungs. The yang dragon emerges from the palace of li and the yin tiger emerges from the palace of k'an. When the five elements follow the cycle of creation, the vapor is transferred from the mother to the son. Thus, from tzu [11:00 p.m.] to wu [11:00 a.m.], yang is born within yang. When the five elements follow the reverse cycle, the flow of the liquid is governed by the husband-wife relationship. Thus, from wu (11:00 a.m.] to tzu [11:00 p.m.], yang is refined within yin. Yang is incomplete without yin. Eventually, when there is no yin, you will not die. Yin cannot be born without yang. Eventually, when yin is completely purged, you will attain longevity."

Lü asked:

"The five elements are made up of yin and yang vapors. What does it mean that they are all directed by one vapor?"

Chung said:

"The one vapor emerges when our father and mother copulate. Generative fluid and blood interact to create form. In the formation of the fetus, the spleen emerges from the kidneys, the liver emerges from the spleen, the lungs emerge from the liver, the heart emerges from the lungs, the small intestines emerge from the heart, the large intestine emerges from the small intestines, the gall bladder emerges from the large intestine, the stomach emerges from the gall bladder, and the bladder emerges from the stomach. All the internal organs are created from the interaction of generative fluid and blood. Everything starts from the first emergence of yang. The one yang is embodied in the two kidneys and the kidneys belong to the element water. In water there is fire. When the water rises, it is called vapor. When vapor ascends, it will move toward the heart. The heart is yang in nature. When yang meets yang, the Great Ultimate will give birth to yin. When the vapor of yin accumulates, fluid will emerge. The fluid descends from the heart, and in its descent it will return to the kidneys. The liver is the mother of the heart and the son of the kidneys; it directs the vapor from the kidneys to the heart. The lungs are the wife of the heart and the mother of the kidneys; they direct the fluid from the heart to the kidneys. The rise and fall of the vapor and the fluid follow the behavior of yin and yang in the sky and the earth. The liver and the lungs also direct their vapors in accordance with the behavior of the sun and the moon.

"The five elements are simply a convenient way of talking about the numerics of creation. In actual fact, creation and interaction both originate from the undifferentiated vapor of the primordial yang. Fluid is born within vapor and vapor is born within fluid. The kidneys are the root of the vapor and the heart is the origin of the fluid. When the spirit is strong and stable, subtly and elusively, the true water will emerge within the vapor. When the source of the heart is pure and clear, quietly and mysteriously the true fire will emerge within the fluid. Understand the true dragon and know how to draw it out of the fire; recognize the true tiger and know how to extract it from the water. When the dragon and the tiger copulate, they will be transformed into the yellow sprouts. When the yellow sprouts mature, the great medicine will be completed and the golden pill will materialize, and when you attain the golden pill, you will become an immortal."

Lü asked:

"You have told me that when we attain the golden pill, we can shed our shells, rise to immortality, and return to the ten islands. Can you tell me what the yellow sprouts are?"

Chung said:

"They are the true dragon and the true tiger."

Lü asked:

"What are the dragon and the tiger?"

Chung said:

"The dragon is not the dragon in the liver; it is the yang dragon that emerges from the true water in the palace of li. The tiger is not the tiger of the lungs; it is the yin tiger that emerges from the true fire in the palace of k'an."

7

Fire and Water

Lü said:

"We can attain longevity if we can cultivate the golden pill. However, to cultivate the golden pill, we must first gather the yellow sprouts, and to gather the yellow sprouts, we must obtain the dragon and the tiger. The true dragon emerges from the palace of li and the true tiger emerges from the palace of k'an. Within k'an and li are water and fire. Can you tell me about this water and fire?"

Chung said:

"The waters in the human body are these: the four seas, the five lakes, the nine rivers, and the three islands. These are some of the names that have been given to them: hua-chih (Radiant Pool), yao-chih (Green Pool), feng-chih (Phoenix Pool), t'ien-chih (Celestial Pool), yü-chih (Jade Pool), k'un-chih (Pool of the K'un-lun Mountains), yüan-tan (Primordial Deep Pool), lang-yüan (Immortals' Terrace), shen-shui (Sacred Water), chin-po (Golden Waves), ch'iung-i (Red Fluid), yü-chuan (Jade Spring), yang-su (Milk of the Sun), and pai-hsüeh (White Snow).

"The fires in the human body are these: the ruling fire, the subordinate fire, and the common fire. The three fires origi-

nate from the primordial yang. Together they give birth to
the true vapor. If the true vapor accumulates, you will feel
peaceful and healthy. If the true vapor is weak, you will be ill.
If the true vapor escapes, the primordial yang will be lost.
When the primordial yang is completely dissipated, pure yin
will dominate. When the primordial spirit (yüan-shen) leaves
the body, you will die."

Lü said:

"In our body the one spark of the primordial yang can generate the three fires. However, the three fires come from
sources of water that are yin. Thus the primordial yang is easy
to lose and difficult to accumulate. As a result, yang will be
weak and yin will be strong. Thus the fires will be small and
the waters will be expansive. If this is the case, we will age
swiftly and never be able to attain longevity. How can we
overcome this problem?"

Chung said:

"The heart is the sea of blood, the kidneys are the sea of
vapor, the brain is the sea of marrow, and the spleen and stomach are the sea of the waters of the seed. These are the four
seas in the body. The five viscera each have their storage of
fluid. They are the manifestations of the five directions east,
west, south, north, and center. These are the five lakes. The
small intestines measure two [Chinese] cubits and four [Chi-
nese] feet. [One Chinese cubit equals ten Chinese feet.] Because there are nine loops above and nine below, the small
intestines are called the nine rivers. Below the small intestines
is the yüan-tan (Primordial Deep Pool). The head is the upper
island, the heart is the middle island, and the kidneys form
the lower island. The root and foundation of the three islands
is the lang-yüan (Immortals' Terrace). The hua-chih (Radiant
Pool) is located below the huang-ting (Yellow Chamber). The
yao-chih (Green Pool) is at the opening of the cavity of the
elixir. The k'un-chih (Pool of the K'un-lun Mountains) is connected above to the yü-chih (Jade Pool). The t'ien-chih (Celestial Pool) flows straight into the Inner Chamber. The feng-

chih (Phoenix Pool) lies between the heart and the lungs. The yü-chih (Jade Pool) lies in the area of the lips and the teeth. The shen-shui (Sacred Water) is born within the vapor. The chin-po (Golden Waves) descends from the sky. Where the red dragon resides, you will find the ch'iung-i (Red Fluid) and yü-chuan (Jade Spring). When the fetus is formed, you will see the yang-su (the Milk of the Sun) and the pai-hsüeh (White Snow).

"If you nourish and nurture the fetus on schedule and apply moisture to help it grow, you will first attain the jade liquid and then the golden liquid. At this time you will be able to circulate the elixir. If you replenish and gather in conjunction with bathing and steaming in the middle and lower tant'iens (elixir fields), you will be able to cultivate the body. The jade medicine and golden fire will be transformed into yellow and white. If you refine the red wine and jade nectar, they will be transformed into a substance with an exquisite fragrance. All these processes are based on the correct application of water.

"When the common fire ascends, it will help the vapor of the kidneys to create the true water. When the fire of the kidneys rises to interact with the fluid of the heart, true vapor will be born. Accumulate a small amount and you will be able to subdue monsters and cure illness. Accumulate a large amount and you will be able to refine the substance and heat the pill.

"When you apply the microcosmic fire, your body will feel hot. At this time you must close the gate of yang so that the medicine can be refined. Pattern the incubator after the form of the nine continents and nurture the yang spirit in it. Burn the three monsters and get rid of the yin ghosts. Circulate the fire upward to penetrate the three gates; circulate the fire downward to grind and dissolve the seven souls. When form is refined and transmuted into vapor, the body will become light and you will be able to fly. When vapor is refined and transmuted into spirit, you will be able to shed your shell. All these processes are based on the correct application of fire."

Lü said:

"At first I was of the impression that the weakness of fire and the overwhelming strength of water would present an unsolvable problem. Now, after hearing your explanations, I understand that water and fire each have their own functions. Can you tell me how to increase that which is small and strengthen that which is weak?"

Chung said:

"Yin wanes in the numerics of two and eight and yang waxes in the numerics of nine and three. Understand this and you will see the completion of the dazzling red-golden pill. When the seven is circulated and the nine returns, you will be able to shed your shell and become an immortal. The true vapor is in the heart. The heart is the source of the liquid, the kidneys are the sea of vapor, and the bladder is the common fire. Applying the common fire is not enough; the bladder must also be able to store saliva and fluid. If the followers of the Tao do not understand the workings of heaven and if they try to guess and approximate the subtle principles, they will find it hard to attain the transformations. Worse, they may get sick and die."

Lü asked:

"The transformations help yang grow and make yin disappear. How can we realize the golden pill, shed our shells, and become immortals?"

Chung said:

"In the body the heart and the kidneys are separated by eight and four-tenths [Chinese] inches. The distance between them parallels the distance between the sky and the earth. In the Great Ultimate, when yin and yang copulate, vapor and fluid will mutually create each other. There are twelve two-hour partitions in each day. These partitions parallel the twelve months of the year. The heart creates fluid. However, it cannot do it alone. In order for the fluid to emerge from the heart, the fluid of the lungs must descend to direct the fluid out of the heart. When the flow of the fluid follows the husband-wife relationship, it will first move up and then down to return to the lower tan-t'ien. This process is called 'the wife returning to the palace of the husband.' The kidneys create vapor. However, they cannot do it alone. In order for the vapor to emerge from the kidneys, the vapor of the bladder must rise to direct the vapor out of the kidneys. When the flow of the vapor follows the mother-son relationship, it will first move down and then up to gather at the middle tan-t'ien. This process is called 'the husband returning to the palace of the wife.' The vapor of the liver directs the vapor of the kidneys. The vapor first flows down and then up toward the heart. The heart is fire, and when the two vapors interact, the lungs will be bathed in steam. When the fluid of the lungs descends to the heart, the fluid of the heart is created. When this fluid emerges and does not leak out of the body, it is called the true water. The fluid of the lungs directs the fluid of the heart. The fluid first flows upward and then down to the kidneys. The kidneys are water, and when the two waters interact, the bladder will be immersed in moisture. When the vapor of the bladder rises to the kidneys, the vapor of the kidneys is created. When this vapor emerges and does not escape from the body, it is called the true fire.

"The true fire emerges from water. It is elusive and subtle. Although it has substance, it cannot be seen. Even if you try to hold on to it, you will not be able to keep it. The true water emerges from fire. It is quiet and mysterious. Although it has essence, it cannot be retained. Even if you try to retain it, it will escape."

Lü said:

"The kidneys belong to the element water. Vapor born in the water is called the true fire. What is the substance that is contained within the fire? The heart belongs to the element fire. Fluid that is born in the fire is called the true water. What is the essence that is contained within the water? The sub-

69

stance in the fire and the essence in the water have no form and are intangible. To begin with, they are difficult to obtain. However, if we obtained them, how should they be applied?"

Chung said:

"Followers of the Tao past and present have all relied on these two substances to attain immortality. The two substances copulate to produce the yellow sprouts. When the numerics of the fetus are complete, the great medicine will be realized. These two substances are the true dragon and the true tiger."

8

Dragon and Tiger

Lü said:

"The dragon is the primordial form of the liver and the tiger is the spirit of the lungs. The fluid that emerges from the fire of the heart is the true water. Quietly and mysteriously, it hides the true dragon in the water. Why do you say that the dragon does not come from the liver but resides in the palace of li? The vapor that emerges from the kidneys is the true vapor. Subtly and elusively, it hides the tiger within the true fire. Why do you say that the tiger does not come from the lungs but resides in the palace of k'an?"

Chung said:

"The dragon is yang in nature. It flies in the sky, and when it roars, clouds are born and the ten thousand things are moistened. Its primal form is the green dragon; its directions are chia and i [east]; its element is wood; its season is spring; and in the ways of humanity, it represents benevolence. Its trigram is chen, and in the body it is the liver. The tiger is yin in nature. It runs on the ground, and when it cries, winds blow in the mountains and all the insects are subdued. Its primal form is the white tiger; its directions are keng and hsin [west]; its element is metal; its season is autumn; and in the ways of humanity, it represents integrity and honor. Its trigram is tui, and in the body it is the lungs.

"Although the liver is yang in nature, it resides in the position of yin. The vapor of the kidneys feeds the vapor of the liver. Following the mother-son relationship, water gives birth to wood. When the vapor of the kidneys is plentiful, the vapor of the liver will be strong. When the vapor of the liver is strong, the remaining yin in the kidneys will be purged and the vapor of pure yang will rise. Although the lungs are yin in nature, they reside in the position of yang. The fluid of the heart feeds the fluid of the lungs. Following the husband-wife relationship, fire tames metal. When the fluid of the heart reaches the lungs, the fluid of the lungs is born. When the fluid of the lungs emerges, the remaining yang in the heart will be purged and the fluid of pure yin will descend.

"The liver is yang in nature and can rid the kidneys of yin. The vapor that passes through the liver is pure yang. Hidden within the vapor of pure yang is the one true water. Intangible and formless, it is called the yang dragon. The lungs are yin in nature and can rid the heart of yang. The fluid that flows into the lungs is the pure yin. Hidden within the fluid of pure yin is the vapor of the true yang. Elusive and invisible, it is called the yin tiger.

"Vapor rises and fluid descends, so normally the two do not interact. However, when the one true water in the vapor meets the fluid, the two will join, and when the true yang in the fluid encounters the vapor, they will be bonded. If you know how to use the correct methods to control the vapor and the fluid when they interact, so that the vapor of the kidneys does not escape and the one true water can be harvested from the vapor, then the fluid of the heart will not leak out. In this way you will be able to gather the vapor of the true yang from the fluid. The mother and son will unite and will mutually care for each other. The rice will receive the rays of the sun and grow. If nothing goes wrong in your cultivation, the medicine will mature in a hundred days. In two hundred days the sacred fetus will be formed, and in three hundred days you will be able to shed your shell and become an immortal.

"The golden pill is shaped like the egg of a cicada and is red-orange in color. When it stands guard in the lower tan-t'ien, you will be able to preserve your body, live forever in the earthly realm, and become an earth immortal."

Lü said:

"Vapor is born from the waters of the kidneys. Within the vapor is the one true water, which is called the yin tiger. When the tiger and the fluid meet, they will join together. Fluid is born from the fire of the heart. Within the fluid is the one true yang, which is called the yang dragon. When the dragon and vapor meet, they will be bonded. Things that are attracted to each other will join and things that are different will move off into their own group. This is the normal way of things. Thus, when vapor emerges, won't the one true water in the vapor follow the path of the fluid and descend into the five viscera? And when the liquid emerges, won't the one true yang follow the path of the vapor and rise to the multileveled pagoda? If the true water follows the downward flow of the fluid, then the tiger will not be able to interact with the dragon. If the true yang follows the upward flow of the vapor, then the dragon will not be able to interact with the tiger. If the dragon and the tiger do not interact, how can the yellow sprouts emerge? If there are no yellow sprouts, how can the great medicine be realized?"

Chung said:

"When the vapor of the kidneys emerges, it is like the sun rising from the sea. Neither fog nor cloud can hide its light. Compared with the vapor, the fluid flowing downward is but a bamboo window shade. How can the descending fluid block the force of the vapor? If the vapor is strong, the one true water will also be strong. When the fluid of the heart emerges, it is as fierce as the winter sky that kills all things. Nothing can oppose its chill. Compared with the fluid, the vapor flowing upward is like a moth. How can the rising vapor battle the strength of the fluid? If the fluid is strong, the true yang will also be strong. However, the strength of these substances will vary among practitioners."

Lü said:

"Vapor and fluid are born at particular times. At the moment the vapor is born, both the vapor and the one true water within it are strong. At the moment the fluid is born, both the fluid and the true yang within it are strong. Why do you say that the strength of these substances will vary among practitioners?"

Chung said:

"The vapor of the kidneys leaks out easily; therefore it is difficult to obtain the true tiger. The fluid of the heart does not accumulate easily; therefore it is difficult to hold on to the true dragon. Thousands of volumes of scriptures have discussed the workings of yin and yang, but the workings of yin and yang are none other than the natures of the dragon and the tiger. Many practitioners do not understand this because their knowledge is based on hearsay and gossip. They only know about the principle of the interaction of the dragon and the tiger; they do not know when the two should copulate and when the products of the interaction should be gathered. This is why many practitioners can only enjoy the small benefits of cultivation. They are able to lengthen their years but they cannot shed their shells. The main reason for their failure is that they are unable to bring together the dragon and the tiger. When the dragon and the tiger do not copulate, the yellow sprouts cannot emerge, and when the yellow sprouts cannot be gathered, the elixir medicine cannot be realized."

9

The Medicines

Lü said:

"I now understand the principles of the dragon and the tiger. Can you tell me more about the golden pill and the great medicine?"

Chung said:

"A medicine is something that can cure illness. There are three kinds of illnesses. First, if you get sick from sleeping in wet clothes in a draughty room, or from exposing yourself to extreme heat and cold, or from working too hard and tiring yourself, or from not eating properly, you will suffer from what is called the illnesses of the seasons. Second, if you do not cultivate [the Tao] and if you follow the desires of your heart, you will lose the primordial yang, dissipate the true vapor, and age swiftly. This is called the illness of aging. Third, if your form is emptied of vapor and if the spirit is gone, your body will have no ruler and you will die. After you have breathed your last, you will lie rigid in the ground in the wilderness. This is death, and death is the illness of the body.

"There are also illnesses of the seasons that occur specifically in spring, summer, autumn, and winter. These illnesses are associated with cold, hot, warm, and cool weather. Illnesses caused by too much yang and not enough yin can be cured by introducing coolness. Illnesses caused by too much yin and not enough yang can be cured by introducing warmth. Older people typically suffer from cold and infants typically suffer from heat. Obese people have too much saliva and thin people have too much intestinal residue. Men get sick from loss of vapor and women get sick from loss of blood. To cure these types of illnesses, we need to fill that which is empty, hold on to that which is substantive, strengthen the weaknesses, and replenish that which has been lost. If the problem is small, we can use acupuncture or herbal medicine. Even if you suffer from the illnesses of the seasons frequently, you can be cured with the help of a skillful doctor and the appropriate herbs.

"How do we cure the illnesses of aging and death? Skillful doctors in the ancient times could wash and clean your intestines and repair damages to the skin. However, no one knows how to return people with wrinkled skin and white hairs to their youth. Skillful doctors in the ancient times could perform head surgery and mend broken bones. However, no one knows how to preserve the body and attain longevity."

Lü asked:

"Illnesses of the seasons can be taken care of by good doctors and high-quality medicine. Are there medicines that can cure the illnesses of aging and death?"

Chung said:

"Of the three kinds of illnesses, the illnesses of the seasons can be cured by herbs and plant extracts. The illnesses of aging and death, however, can be cured only by two special types of medicines. The first type is called the internal pill and the second type is called the external pill."

Lü asked:

"What is the external pill?"

Chung said:

"When the primordial lord on high transmitted the teachings of the Tao to humanity, he taught us the principles of the rise and fall of the vapors of the sky and the earth and described to us the cyclical course of the sun and the moon. Consequently many texts were written about the pill and people got to know about the Great Tao. The sage Kuang-ch'eng Tzu taught the Yellow Emperor. The Yellow Emperor cultivated himself in his spare time but achieved nothing. Then Kuang-ch'eng Tzu told him that true vapor and true water lie in the heart and the kidneys and true yin and true yang lie within the vapor and the water. When combined, they form the great medicine. Rare and precious as gold hidden deep inside the rocks, they are found in the hollow caves in the mountains. Using techniques of the bedchamber, these substances can be tempered and refined into the great elixir. Of the eight kinds of stones, only red cinnabar is used. From cinnabar, mercury is extracted. Of the five minerals, only black lead is used. From lead, silver is extracted. The mercury is analogous to the yang dragon and the silver is analogous to the yin tiger. The color of red cinnabar is likened to the fire of the heart and the color of black lead is likened to the waters of the kidneys. The yearly schedule of stoking the fire follows the behavior of ch'ien and k'un; the monthly gathering requires applying the scholar and the warrior fires. The furnace has three levels, each level measuring nine [Chinese] inches. Externally it is angular; internally it is round. The furnace draws in the vapors of the eight directions, it is in harmony with the movement of the four seasons, and it is shaped like a golden cauldron. Hiding the lead and mercury within, it is analogous to the lungs that produce the fluid. Sulfur is the medicine, and when compounded with the numinous cinnabar, it is analogous to the Yellow Woman.

"After three years of alchemical work, you will obtain a pill that will produce a small effect. If you ingest this pill, all your illnesses will be cured. After six years of alchemical work, you will obtain a pill that will produce a moderate effect. If you ingest this pill, you will achieve longevity. After nine years of alchemical work, you will obtain a pill that will produce a large effect. If you ingest this pill, you will be able to fly and travel tens of thousands of miles. Although you cannot return to the immortal islands of Peng-lai, you will be able to escape death and live forever in the earthly realm."

Lü asked:

"In the past, many have tried to cultivate the pill but few have succeeded. Why is this so?"

Chung said:

"There are three reasons why people have failed to cultivate the pill. First, they could not distinguish between the real medicines and the false ones. Furthermore, they did not know how to apply the fire and gather the substances. As a result, they burned the precious substances to ashes. Confused about the schedules of firing, they wasted their effort for nothing. Second, there are those who had high-quality medicines but did not know how to apply the fire, and those who understood the schedules of firing but had low-quality medicines. These practitioners failed because they were unable to compound the substances. Third, there are those who had good medicines and knew the schedule of firing. In following the yearly schedule they did not miss a month, and in following the monthly schedule they never missed a day. They understood when to add and when to subtract and knew the times of flow and ebb. The vapor was sufficient and the pill materialized, but they were unprepared to circulate it. As a result, the mysterious crane disappeared into thin air, and they lost their chance to ingest the pill.

"The medicines are the essences of the sky and the earth. The schedules of applying fire are transmitted by the immortals. In the period of the three kings, the Yellow Emperor completed the pill after nine cycles of circulation. After the period of the five emperors, three years of alchemical work were needed before the pill would materialize. During the years of the Warring States, the scent of death filled the air and spread across the nation. Nature could no longer absorb the essences of the sky and the earth to produce the exquisite medicines.

Those who knew the formulas fled to the remote mountains and deep valleys and died with the knowledge locked inside them. The bamboo strips on which the methods have been recorded have disintegrated. As a result, the methods of compounding the pill were lost to the world.

"If the medicines are still available in the world, then why did the emperor of Ch'in send an expedition overseas to search for the islands of immortality? If the formulas for compounding the elixir are known to the world, then why did Wei Po-yang need to rediscover the methods by studying the theory of change? Do not trust people who advertise that they know the methods. It is likely that they got the information through rumors and hearsay. These false teachers mislead future generations, bring destruction to families, harm their students, and accomplish nothing for themselves. You won't find the medicines in the world, and those who continue to try to find them externally are only wasting their time."

Lü said:

"The principles of the external pill originated from Kuang-ch'eng Tzu. Using the techniques of the bedchamber, he managed to get some results after nine years of cultivation. It is hard enough to find the medicines, and it is even harder to obtain the formulas. Even if we had succeeded in compounding the pill, we could only fly up to the sky—we could not transcend the mundane, enter the sacred, and return to the ten continents. Therefore it seems that we have no choice but to work with the internal medicines. Can you tell me how to obtain them?"

Chung said:

"It is wrong to say that we should not use external medicines. Those who begin their cultivation in their old age do not have strong foundations. The kidneys are the root of the vapor, and if the roots are not deep, the leaves will not be healthy. The heart is the source of the fluid, and if the source is not clear, the fluid cannot last. Therefore older people must first use the five minerals and the eight stones to help them start their cultivation. With time they will be able to refine the three substances. Each substance has three categories. Together they are called 'the nine categories of the great dragon-tiger elixir.' This elixir will reconnect them with the true vapor. It will help them refine their form so that they can live a long life on earth, and it will also make their bodies light so that they can fly.

"If they continue to cultivate using the techniques of the bedchamber, if they know the best time to copulate, and if they know how to gather the ingredients, with time they will be able to shed their shells and become immortals. However, if you think that you can enter the celestial realm by holding on to the external pill and applying fire to it daily, then you are mistaken, because this is not how the external medicines work.

"Now I will tell you about the principles of the internal pill. The medicines of the internal pill come from the kidneys. Everyone has them. The medicines of the internal pill are also found in the sky and the earth. If the schedule of firing follows the numerics of the cycles of the sun and the moon, and if the method of interaction is patterned after the copulation between the male and the female, the sacred fetus will materialize and the true vapor will be born. Like a pearl growing inside a dragon, vapor will emerge within the vapor. When the great medicine is realized, the yang spirit will appear. Another body will emanate from the body, like a cicada coming out of its cocoon. This is the internal pill. It originates from the copulation of the dragon and the tiger. When the dragon and the tiger copulate, they will be transformed into the yellow sprouts. When the yellow sprouts mature, lead and mercury will separate."

10

Lead and Mercury

Lü said:

"The internal medicine is nothing but the dragon and the tiger. The tiger is born in the palace of k'an: it is the water within the vapor. The dragon emerges from the palace of li: it is the vapor within the water. In the external medicine, the mercury extracted from the cinnabar is equivalent to the yang dragon, and the silver extracted from the lead is equivalent to the yin tiger. Lead and mercury are both external medicines. How can their equivalents, the dragon and the tiger, copulate and become the yellow sprouts? When the yellow sprouts emerge, lead and mercury will separate. What are the equivalents of lead and mercury in the internal medicine?"

Chung said:

"The black lead embodies the one substance of heaven and occupies the highest place among the five metals. Lead gives birth to silver; thus lead is the mother of silver. The red cinnabar receives the vapor of the sun and occupies the highest place among stones. Cinnabar gives birth to mercury; thus cinnabar is the mother of mercury. It is difficult to extract silver from lead and it is difficult to prevent mercury from escaping out of the cinnabar. However, when silver and mercury combine, they can be refined into the most precious substance. These are the principles of lead and mercury as manifested externally in nature.

"With reference to the use of generative energy in human reproduction, there are many theories. Let's just say that seminal fluid and blood interact in the most subtle and mysterious ways when our father and mother copulate. The true vapor is stored within the palace of pure yang in the mother's womb, and the spirit is kept in the place where yin and yang have not differentiated. In three hundred days the fetus will be mature, and in five thousand days it will be filled with vapor.

"With reference to the five elements, it is known that the human body is created from generative fluid and blood. Thus, first there is water. With reference to the five viscera, generative fluid and blood are but manifestations. In a fetus the kidneys emerge first, because the waters in the kidneys are already there when the fetus is conceived. The true vapor of our father and mother is hidden in the internal kidneys [the testes]. This is lead. Vapor is ruled by the kidneys, and the one true water in the vapor is called the true tiger or the silver within the lead. The vapor of the kidneys is directed to the vapor of the liver, and the vapor of the liver is directed to the vapor of the heart. In the Great Ultimate, the vapor of the heart gives birth to the fluid. Within the fluid is the vapor of true yang. The fluid of the heart is the red cinnabar, and mercury is the vapor of the true yang within the fluid. When the one true water in the vapor is attracted to and is in harmony with the vapor of true yang in the fluid, vapor and fluid will accumulate and the fetus will be formed. When the fetus moves into the Yellow Chamber and fire is applied appropriately, it will be transformed into the immortal infant. This is why we say that when the silver in the lead is merged with mercury, the most precious substance can be refined."

Lü said:

"With reference to the five metals, we extract silver from lead, and with reference to the eight stones, we extract mercury from cinnabar. These are the medicines that we put inside the cauldron. Mercury originates in cinnabar, and silver is considered as the precious substance. However, internally how do we extract silver from lead? Within the body, how do we obtain the cinnabar, and how can we extract mercury from it? And why is silver regarded as a precious substance?"

Chung said:

"Lead is the true vapor of our father and mother. Originally joined together, these substances never leave each other. When they take on form, they are stored in the kidneys. The two kidneys work together to drive the vapor upward. This vapor is the vapor of the primordial yang. Within the vapor is water, which is called the one true water. Water rises together with vapor. When vapor stops moving, the water will also stop moving. When the vapor leaks out, the water will also leak out. Water and vapor are intertwined like mother and son. Even experienced practitioners can feel only the vapor—they cannot feel the water. When this one true water merges with the true vapor of the heart, the process is referred to as 'the dragon and the tiger copulating to become the yellow sprouts.' With time the yellow sprouts will be transformed into the great medicine. Thus the ingredients of the great medicine are embodied in the one true water that forms the womb and encloses the true vapor of yang. The creation of the immortal fetus is likened to the creation of the human fetus: it emerges when the true vapors of the father and mother interact and when the generative fluid and blood are joined. After three hundred days the fetus will be mature and filled with vapor. When the form is ready, the spirit will descend and the fetus will be separated from the mother. In this way form and spirit are united, and also in this way, form has created another form.

"In the body of the practitioner, the vapor of the kidneys interacts with the vapor of the heart. The one true water in the vapor carries with it the one true vapor. When the vapor interacts with the one true water, the fetus is conceived. The embryo is shaped like a grain of rice and it must be steamed and nurtured. In the beginning you should use yin to hold on to the yang. Then you should use yang to refine the yin. In due process the vapor will be transformed into generative fluid, the generative fluid will be transformed into mercury, the mercury will be transformed into cinnabar grains, and the cinnabar grains will be transformed into the golden pill. When the golden pill materializes, the true vapor will be born. If you refine the vapor into spirit, you will be able to transcend the mundane. Transformed into the fire dragon, you will emerge from the undifferentiated radiance; merged with the mysterious crane, you will enter the immortals islands of Peng-lai."

Lü said:

"When form interacts with form, form will create another form. When vapor interacts with vapor, vapor will create vapor. In human reproduction the forms [mother and child] separate after three hundred days, and male and female infants take on different physiological characteristics. However, in the internal transformations, there is only one manifestation of the grains of the pill: they are moist and shiny. Why is this so?"

Chung said:

"During copulation, if the generative fluid of the father enters the womb before the blood of the mother, the blood will embrace the fluid and a female fetus will be formed. The form of the female is structured after the mother: yin encloses yang and the blood is on the outside. However, if the blood of the mother enters the womb before the generative fluid of the father, the fluid will embrace the blood and a male fetus will be formed. The form of the male is structured after the father: yang encloses yin and the fluid is on the outside.

"The blood originates in the heart and does not embody the true vapor of yang. The generative fluid, however, originates in the kidneys and has in it the true vapor of yang. The true vapor of yang is the essence of mercury: it is the one true water. The true vapor should be harmonized and brought into the Yellow Chamber. Inside the Yellow Chamber, mercury will be steamed and stirred by the lead while lead will be heated by the fire of the mercury. If lead does not encounter mercury, it will not be able to produce the one true water, and if mercury does not encounter lead, it cannot be transformed into the vapor of pure yang."

Lü said:

"Lead in the kidneys gives birth to the vapor of primordial yang, and out of the vapor the one true water emerges. This substance is invisible and intangible. Mercury has in it the vapor of true yang. Coming into contact with lead, the vapor of true yang will heat the lead and refine it. When lead is nourished, the vapor will be strong and the one true water will be produced and driven upward. Now, mercury is originally the vapor of true yang. It is the one true water that encloses the fetus. When it is brought into the Yellow Chamber, the dragon and the tiger will copulate, and both yin and yang will stop circulating. If we use lead to steam and stir the mercury, won't there be too much yin? If there is too much yin, won't the true yang escape? And if the true yang escapes, how can the great medicine be realized?"

Chung said:

"When the vapor of the kidneys moves toward the vapor of the heart, the vapor will wax strong and produce the fluid. When the true yang within the vapor encounters the one true water, the process is called 'the dragon copulating with the tiger.' After the dragon and the tiger copulate, with time the rice will grow. This is the great medicine of the golden pill. After the pill emerges, it must be brought into the Yellow Chamber. Where is the Yellow Chamber? It is below the spleen and the stomach and above the bladder. It is north of the heart, south of the kidneys, west of the liver, and east of the lungs. [In the Chinese compass, south is on top.] It is clear on top and muddy at the bottom. Externally it takes on the four colors. When it is full it is linked to the two ascending pathways and connected with the eight channels of water.

Medicine that you have gathered will stay there day and night.

"If you gather the medicine and do not apply fire, the medicine will dissipate. If you apply fire but do not gather the medicine, the yang within the yin will escape. Under these circumstances, the best you can hope for is to produce vapor from the kidneys and use it to strengthen and warm the lower primordial region.

"If you want to gather the medicine at the appropriate time and if you want to apply the fire according to the correct numerics, you must first collect the lead. Stoke the fire with vapor and strengthen the foundation of the medicine. Then, using the method of gathering, let the medicine guard the lower tan-t'ien. If you can refine the mercury and use it to repair the lower tan-t'ien, you will be able to enjoy a long life and become an earth immortal.

"In gathering the medicine, you must extract the primordial lead the moment the golden sparks fly out behind the navel. The whole purpose of extracting the lead is to use it to replenish the mercury. If you do not replenish the mercury, then you will not be able to direct the generative fluid to return to the head. If the generative fluid does not return to the head, how can the true vapor be born? If the true vapor is not born, how can the yang spirit be realized? Therefore, if you want to replenish the mercury, you must extract the lead. If you do not extract the lead, you will not be able to refine the mercury and repair the tan-t'ien. If the tan-t'ien is not repaired, how can the mercury be crystallized into cinnabar grains? If the cinnabar grains are not transmuted, how can the golden pill be realized?"

11

Extracting and Replenishing

Lü said:

"We rely on the water in the vapor to gather the medicine, but before we can apply the fire, we must obtain the vapor in the lead. Therefore, if we are to realize the great medicine, we will need to extract the lead. If we only replenish the mercury but do not extract the lead, we can only hope to repair the lower tan-t'ien. Can you tell me how to extract the lead and use it to replenish the mercury?"

Chung said:

"In the ancient times, the sacred ones on high wanted to transmit the teachings of the Tao to humanity. Our ancestors lived simple lives, had few desires, knew little about the things in the world, and had no idea of what the Tao is about. However, they were aware of the rise and fall of the vapors in the sky and the earth and they knew that the vapors of warmth, coolness, cold, and hot shaped the seasons. There is a time for every season, and the duration of each season is determined by the numerics of the year. When one cycle ends, the next one begins. This is why the sky and the earth can last forever.

"Consider the waxing and waning of the essences of the sun and the moon. The principles of flow and ebb are manifested in the four phases of the moon: new, first quarter, full, and last quarter moon. Rising and setting, waxing and waning, the moon gives each month its full complement of days. The months and the years continue without fail because they follow the principles of the Tao. It is also why the sun and the moon can last forever.

"Summer's heat is followed by winter's cold, and winter's cold is followed by summer's heat. People nowadays do not understand this simple principle of the rise and fall of vapors in the sky and the earth. The full moon is followed by a sickle moon and the sickle moon is followed by a full moon. Today people are ignorant of this principle of the movement of the sun and the moon. As a result, they waste their limited time on earth chasing after pleasures and desires. They do not understand that luxuries and riches are like fleeting clouds and they do not realize that attachment and anxiety sow seeds of karmic retribution in the next lifetime. Before the songs of pleasure end, they are already sad; while they savor fame and fortune, their youth and good looks have slipped away. Greedy for material goods, they have doomed themselves to karmic disasters. Attached to children and grandchildren, they want to be with their family forever. Desiring a long life, they entertain false hopes of attaining longevity, not knowing that they have squandered their primordial yang by letting the true vapor escape. The day they curb their desires is when they become severely ill, and the day they stop their bad habits is when they meet death.

"The true immortals and the sacred beings on high took pity on humankind. Not wanting to see us sunk into countless cycles of reincarnation, they taught us about the Great Tao, told us about the principles of the rise and the fall of yin and yang in the sky and the earth, and explained to us the principles of the waxing and waning of the essences of the sun and the moon. Great as the sky and the earth and bright as the sun and the moon, the essences are manifested externally as metals and stones. Internally they are manifested as vapor and fluid. If we want to gather them, we must replenish them, and if we want to replenish them, we must extract them. The principle of extracting and replenishing lies at the root of all creation and transformation.

"After the winter solstice, yang rises from the earth and yin is extracted from the ground. When the great yin is extracted, emerging [incomplete] yin is born. In this process lesser yang is replenished and is transformed into bright yang. When emerging yin is extracted, lesser yin is born. In this process bright yang is replenished and is transformed into great yang. If extracting and replenishing do not occur, then cold will not be transformed into warmth and warmth will not be transformed into heat. After the summer solstice, yin descends from the sky and yang is extracted from heaven. When the great yang is extracted, bright yang emerges. In this process lesser yin is replenished and is transformed into emerging yin. When bright yang is extracted, lesser yang emerges. In this process emerging yin is replenished and is transformed into great yin. If extracting and replenishing do not occur, then heat will not be transformed into coolness and coolness will not be transformed into cold. This is how yin and yang in the sky and earth ascend and descend to transform the six vapors of weather. The process is patterned after the principle of extracting and replenishing.

"When the moon receives the spirit of the sun, the sun will become the soul of the moon. In the first fifteen days of the lunar month, the soul is extracted out of the moon to replenish the spirit in the sun. When the moon is filled with essence, its brightness will illuminate the earth. If extracting and replenishing do not occur, then the new moon will not be transformed into the first quarter moon and the first quarter moon will not be transformed into the full moon. When the moon takes back its yin soul, the yang essence will return to the sun. In the last fifteen days of the month, the spirit is extracted out of the sun to replenish the soul in the moon. The light of the moon is spent because its soul is filled with yin. If extracting and replenishing do not occur, then the full moon will not be transformed into the last quarter moon and the last quarter moon will not be transformed into the dark moon. This is how the essences of the sun and the moon wax and wane to transform the nine and the six. This process is also patterned after the principle of extracting and replenishing.

"People do not understand the workings of heaven. They look here and there and try to figure out the subtle principles. The true immortals and the sacred beings saw this and realized that humankind wanted longevity and wished to be free from illness. Therefore they talked about the techniques of the bedchamber and likened them to the methods whereby metals and stones can be transmuted to create the great elixir. Lead and mercury are minerals; therefore they have no feelings. If you can apply the fires on schedule and if you can extract and replenish according to the correct numerics, you will be able to attain the pill and live a long life. However, to let the true yang of the body [which has feelings and emotions] copulate with the one true water at the appropriate time, to understand the methods of gathering, to practice day after day and month after month, to develop vapor within the vapor, to refine the vapor into spirit, and to be liberated from the mundane—these are not easy things to accomplish.

"Many practitioners do not understand the methods. Confused and ignorant about the alchemical work, they have led many astray. Misunderstanding the intentions of the ancient teachers, they extract mercury from cinnabar, mix lead and mercury, use lead to coagulate mercury, and transform mercury into tin. They desire fame and fortune and do not care about life. Goading each other on, they claim that they pursue the Tao, but in actual fact, they are after the benefits of the yellow and the white.

"The lead in our body emerged with the creation of the sky and the earth. Because there is a primal beginning, there is a primal substance, which is the mother of the ten thousand things. Because there is a primal substance, there is a primal purity. These three primal structures are manifested in the metal within the water, and their functions are manifested in the water within the fire. This is the origin of the five elements. Thus the five elements form an integral part of the Great Tao.

"When you gather the medicine, you must replenish the mercury, and when you replenish the mercury, you must extract the lead. This kind of extracting and replenishing does not occur outside the body. Rather, it involves moving something from the lower tan-t'ien to the upper tan-t'ien. The process is called 'letting the golden sparks fly from behind the navel.' It is also referred to as 'starting the Waterwheel to move the dragon and the tiger' and 'attaining longevity by returning the generative fluid to the head.'

"After lead is extracted, mercury will descend from the middle tan-t'ien to the lower tan-t'ien. If you can get the dragon and the tiger to copulate at this time, the two will be transformed into the yellow sprouts. When the five elements interact in their reverse cycle, you should extract the lead, replenish the mercury, and incubate the immortal fetus. This process is called 'stirring and tossing the three tan-t'iens.' If the five elements do not interact in their reverse cycle, the dragon and the tiger will not copulate. Subsequently, the three tan-t'iens cannot be stirred and tossed and the immortal fetus will not be nourished by the vapor.

"After a hundred days of using lead to replenish mercury, the medicine will grow to its full strength. In two hundred days the sacred fetus will be firm. After three hundred days the immortal infant will be mature and the true vapor will be born. When the true vapor emerges, you should refine it and transmute it into the spirit. When you complete the alchemical work, you will be able to transcend your form. When the immortal infant has completed its transformation, you will become a spirit immortal."

Lü said:

"Externally, lead and mercury originate from metals and

stones. If we use the method of extracting and replenishing, we should be able to obtain the precious substance. In our bodies, lead is the true vapor of our mother and father hidden in the kidneys, and mercury is the medicine enclosed in the one true yang. If we use the method of extracting and replenishing, we should be able to compound these two ingredients and create the spirit. Can you tell me how to apply the technique of extracting and replenishing to the true lead and the true mercury?"

Chung said:

"In the beginning you must use lead to obtain mercury. It is a mistake not to use lead to gather the mercury. Extract the lead and direct it into the upper palace, because without lead you will not be able to hold on to the primordial vapor. Once the lead is directed to the upper palace, the generative fluid will enter the head. The mercury obtained from this process will be purely yang and will not have any yin residue in it. The generative energy will be transformed into cinnabar and the cinnabar will be transformed into metal. This metal is the true lead. The true lead is enclosed inside the true vapor and is born within the true vapor. When the one true vapor becomes the five vapors, the five vapors will gather toward the primordial regions, the three yangs will accumulate on top of the head, and the golden essence of generative energy will sink into the lower tan-t'ien. From there the essence will rise again to refine the body. When the body glows with a golden hue, it is a sign that the true lead is rising inside the internal organs. After ten months of alchemical work in the Yellow Chamber and one year of applying the principle of extracting and replenishing, the body will radiate a white light. Moving down and up, up and then down, the elixir will circulate inside to continue to refine the body. The golden essence of the generative energy is now set in motion, and as the elixir circulates from front to back and back to front, the body will feel as if it is heated and immersed in hot vapor. This is a sign that the true vapor is being transmuted. If you only gather the medicine and apply the fire but do not practice the method of extracting and replenishing, you will not be able to achieve these effects."

Lü asked:

"The process of extracting must complement the process of replenishing. What does it mean that up and down, back and forth, the movement follows a course?"

Chung said:

"When it should rise, it must not descend; when it should be extracted, it should not be replenished. There must be no mistake in its movement, whether it is up and down or back and forth. Everything relies on the strength of the Water-wheel."

12

The Waterwheel

Lü asked:

"What is the Waterwheel?"

Chung said:

"In the old days, the wise ones noticed that clouds blocked out the sun and figured out how to build shelters for shade. They saw leaves floating on water and figured out how to build boats. Seeing things swirled by the wind, they intuited the theory of rotation and built the wheel. What is the wheel? It is patterned after the structure of the sky and the earth. The rim is round like the sun and the moon, and when it is rolled on the ground, it can travel across the land.

"Those who understood the principles of the Tao used the concept of the waterwheel to talk about movement in the body. They said that because the body is filled with water, yin dominates yang. Using the images of a wheel to describe movement and a river to describe the waters in the body, they came up with the term waterwheel. This wheel in the body does not travel on land; rather, it moves through water. Ascending and descending, moving backward and forward, it traverses the eight pools and the four seas. Upward it rises to the top of the K'un-lun Mountains; downward it rushes into the Gate of the Phoenix. It circulates the primordial yang between the heart and the lungs and sends it into the palace of li. From there it carries true vapor back to the house of longevity. Swirling in the Yellow Chamber and circling around the nine continents, the Waterwheel is always in motion. Journeying through the three tan-t'iens, it is never at rest.

"When the dragon and the tiger copulate, the Yellow Woman will enter the Yellow Chamber and lead and mercury will be separated. The metal of the male will enter the Golden Tower and move into the Jade Spring in the ni-wan (Mud Ball) cavity. Only half a day of circulation is needed to produce one jar of the golden elixir, and within a fleeting moment, the transfer is completed. If the five elements are not carried by this wheel, how can they be created and nourished? If the one vapor is not carried by this wheel, how can copulation occur inside? If we are to initiate the alchemical processes in accordance with the seasons and the hours, we must use the wheel. Otherwise we will achieve nothing. The process of incubating yang and refining yin also relies on the wheel. Initially, when ch'ien and k'un are not pure, we will need to use the wheel to get yin and yang to interact. When the [internal] universe is incomplete, we will need the wheel to circulate the blood and the vapor. Moving away from the outside to the inside, the wheel circulates the pure yin and pure yang vapors of the sky and the earth and directs them into the home of the primordial yang. Transforming the mundane into the sacred, it circulates the true vapors of yin and yang to repair and refine the house of the primordial spirit (yüan-shen). The things that the Waterwheel can do are amazing."

Lü asked:

"Since the Waterwheel has such tremendous value, can you describe the principles of its movement? What is it in the human body? And if we obtain it, how can it be put to use?"

Chung said:

"The Waterwheel originates in the true waters of the north. The pure vapor that emerges from the true vapor stored in the kidneys is the key to the workings of the wheel. In the past this information was rarely discussed because the true immortals wanted this knowledge to remain secret. When ch'ien seeks out k'un, k'an is born. K'an is water, and water is the essence of yin. When yang encounters yin, yang will carry yin back to its home. In its journey, it will pass through the trigrams ken, chen, and sun. In this process yang is used to attract yin and yin is used to obtain yin. When the yin is brought into li, yang will be born. This is the work of the Waterwheel. It is the vehicle that carries yin into the palace of yang.

"When k'un seeks out ch'ien, li is born. Li is fire, and fire is the essence of yang. When yin encounters yang, yin will embrace the yang and return home with it. In its journey, it will pass through the trigrams k'un, tui, and ch'ien. In this process yin is used to attract yang and yang is used to obtain yang. When the yang is brought into k'an, yin will be born. This is also the work of the Waterwheel. It is the vehicle that carries yang into the palace of yin.

"After the medicine has been gathered above the nine palaces and directed into the Yellow Chamber, and after extracting and replenishing have occurred below the Winding River, the medicine will move up to the Internal Court. It is from here that the jade elixir and golden elixir are circulated. If the wheel is initiated at this time, it will help you to refine your body. Channel the water upward, let the ruling fire and common fire transmute your form, and turn the wheel to heat the pill. If you turn the wheel according to its hourly schedule, the five vapors will move toward the primordial regions. If you turn the wheel according to its daily schedule, the three flowers will accumulate on top of the head. When the spirit is focused, monsters will multiply. If monsters appear, you should use the wheel to direct the true fire to heat the body. When the body is engulfed in flames, the three monsters will disappear. If the medicine is about to wither, you should use the wheel to direct the vapor of the saliva to moisten it. In this way you will be able to dive into the water without a splash. These are the functions of the Waterwheel."

Lü said:

"The Waterwheel originates from the true vapor of the north. It rotates without stopping and is responsible for transporting yin and yang. Each person uses it differently and achieves different results. Honored teacher, can you discuss these things in more detail?"

Chung said:

"The cycle of the five elements follows the principles of reversal silently, the dragon and the tiger copulate, and the yellow sprouts are born—this is the work of the Small Waterwheel. The golden sparks fly up from behind the navel and return to the Mud Ball cavity, lead is extracted to replenish mercury, and the great medicine is realized—this is the work of the Great Waterwheel. When the dragon and the tiger have copulated and lead and mercury have compounded to become the great medicine, the true vapor will be born. When the true vapor emerges, the five vapors will move toward the primordial regions. When the yang spirit is mature, the three spirits will be liberated from the Internal Court. The purple-golden elixir is now complete. The mysterious cranes fly out, the mercurial white jade materializes, and the fire dragon leaps out of its lair. The body is bathed in thousands of rays of golden light. The pearl of the jade tree appears fresh, shiny, and bright; it exits and enters naturally and moves back and forth unhindered. Transporting the spirit into the body, it merges with the primal order and liberates the sacred from the mundane. This is the work of the Purple Waterwheel. These are the three waterwheels. Each waterwheel has its own effect and each effect can be experienced. They are not equivalent to the three vehicles of Buddhism, which are called the Goat Cart, the Deer Cart, and the Great Buffalo Cart.

"In the alchemy of transformation, there are three other wheels besides the Waterwheel. When fire is accumulated, the heart and the intentions will move together to defend the body against illness. This is the work of the Messenger Wheel. When above and below work together, yin and yang will be united, fire and water will be harmonious, and the sound of thunder will be heard in the midst of stillness. This is the work of the Thunder Wheel. However, if the heart is controlled by the external environment and if the mind is led by emotions, we will be affected by things in the world and the vapor of the true yang will dissipate. If we let the vapor leak out of the body and do not rest when we are tired, then with time our energy will be weak, our bodies will be empty, and we will age. The eight evils and five illnesses will corrupt the true vapor and the primordial yang will not be able to oppose them. As a result, we will get old, become ill, and die. These are the effects of the Broken Wheel."

Lü said:

"When the cycle of the five elements reverses and the dragon and the tiger copulate, the Small Waterwheel is in motion. When there is tossing and turning in the three tan-t'iens and the golden sparks fly out from behind the navel, the Great Waterwheel is in motion. How do we know when the Purple Waterwheel is moving?"

Chung said:

"When the followers of the Tao have received instructions from enlightened teachers, they will understand the principles of the rise and fall of vapors in the sky and the earth. As they progress in their cultivation, they will know how to apply the numerics of the waxing and waning of the sun and the moon to introduce yin and yang to each other. With time they will also learn how to accumulate and disseminate water and fire, gather the medicine, apply the fire, and replenish mercury with lead. These are the effects of the Small Waterwheel.

"When the golden sparks fly from behind the navel to the head, the great medicine in the Yellow Chamber will be completed. Thrusting through the three gates, the medicine will enter the Internal Court. That which emerges at the back is harvested in front. Flowing upward, it repairs; flowing downward, it refines. These are signs that the Great Waterwheel is turning.

"When the golden elixir and the jade elixir are circulated to refine the body, when the body is refined and transmuted into vapor, when vapor is refined and transmuted into spirit, and when the spirit is merged with the Tao, the Tao within you will be complete, and you will be able to transcend the mundane and attain immortality. These are signs that the Purple Waterwheel is turning."

13

Returning to the Elixir Fields

Lü said:

"You have said that the body is refined to create vapor, vapor is refined to create spirit, and spirit is refined to be merged with the Tao. You have also said that all these processes begin with 'returning to the elixir.' Can you elaborate on this?"

Chung said:

"The elixir does not have color: we cannot describe it as red or yellow. The elixir does not have flavor: we cannot identify it as sweet or tasty. The elixir is the elixir field (tan-t'ien). There are three tan-t'iens. The upper one is called the abode of the spirit, the middle one is called the house of vapor, and the lower one is called the region of the generative essence. Vapor is born from generative essence and is stored in the middle tan-t'ien; spirit is born from vapor and is stored in the upper tan-t'ien; and the true water and true vapor merge to form the generative essence, which is stored in the lower tan-t'ien. All practitioners have three tan-t'iens. However, if the vapor born in the kidneys does not gather toward the Primordial Middle and if the spirit hidden in the heart does not enter the Upper Court, the generative essence will not be able to return to its home. Thus, even if you have three tan-t'iens, they are useless."

Lü said:

"In the most mysterious way, we are all born with the life force. However, there is no generative essence in it. Technically the vapor does not belong to us: it is the primordial yang of our father and mother. Since we do not have generative essence, we will also not have the vapor. The spirit is not ours either: it is the primordial spirit of our father and mother. Generative essence (ching), vapor (ch'i), and spirit (shen) are the three treasures of the tan-t'iens. How can we make them stay in the upper, middle, and lower palaces?"

Chung said:

"The kidneys create vapor. Within the vapor is the one true water. If the water is returned to the lower tan-t'ien, the numinous roots of the generative essence will be nourished and the vapor will emerge. The heart creates fluid. Within the fluid is the one true vapor of yang. If the true vapor is returned to the middle tan-t'ien, the numinous origin of the vapor will be nurtured and the spirit will emerge. When the numinous spirit is gathered, the primordial spirit will materialize. If you merge the spirit with the Tao and return it to the upper tan-t'ien, you will be liberated from the mundane."

Lü said:

"There are three tan-t'iens—upper, middle, and lower. 'Returning' means going back. The principle of 'returning to the tan-t'iens' is subtle and deep. I would like you to tell me more about it."

Chung said:

"There are many kinds of 'returning.' They are the Minor Return to the elixir field, the Major Return, the Return of the numeric seven, the Circulation and Return of the numeric nine, the Return of the golden elixir, and the Return of the jade elixir. There are also these processes: 'the lower tan-t'ien returning to the upper tan-t'ien,' 'the upper tan-t'ien returning to the lower tan-t'ien,' 'the middle tan-t'ien returning to the lower tan-t'ien,' 'the yang returning to the field of yin,' and 'yin returning to the field of yang.' Each return is unique: they occur at different times and are initiated under different circumstances."

Lü asked:

"What is the Minor Return?"

Chung said:

"The Minor Return originates from the lower tan-t'ien. The lower tan-t'ien rules the five viscera and is the origin of all three tan-t'iens. Water creates wood, wood creates fire, fire creates earth, earth creates metal, and metal creates water. The cycle of creation follows a definite pattern: it uses the created to give birth to the uncreated and is modeled after the mutual caring between mother and son. Fire tames metal, metal tames wood, wood tames earth, earth tames water, and water tames fire. The cycle of taming also follows a set of rules: it uses the tamer to repair the tamed and is patterned after the husband-wife relationship.

"Vapor never stops circulating. Yin and yang are born, respectively, in the hours of wu [11:00 A.M.–1:00 P.M.] and tzu [11:00 P.M.–1:00 A.M.] and are at rest in the hours of mao [5:00–7:00 A.M.] and yu [5:00–7:00 P.M.]. Every twenty-hours [one day and one night] the vapor completes one circulation and returns to the lower tan-t'ien. This is the Minor Return. Practitioners who know how to gather the medicine and apply the fire should be able to build the lower tan-t'ien and achieve the Minor Return."

Lü asked:

"What is the Major Return?"

Chung said:

"The dragon and the tiger copulate and are transformed into the yellow sprouts. Lead is extracted, mercury is replenished, and the great medicine is completed. In the palace of the Black Tortoise, the golden sparks fly up; at the foot of the mountains of the Jade City, the true vapor rises. Carried by the Waterwheel, the vapor climbs to the top of the peak. Along the way it moistens the jade elixir in the middle. The circulation begins with the true vapor flowing from the lower to the upper field. Then it descends from the upper to the lower field. The circulation completes its course when it emerges from the back and arrives at the front. This is the Great Return. Practitioners who know how to get the dragon and the tiger to copulate, eject the golden sparks, nurture the immortal fetus, and create the true vapor should be able to build the middle tan-t'ien and achieve the Major Return."

Lü asked:

"Now that I have heard about the Great Return, can you tell me about the Return of the numeric seven and the Circulation and Return of the numeric nine?"

Chung said:

"In the cycle of the five elements, there are five pairs of numbers in the numerics of creation and completion. Sky is one, three, five, seven, and nine. Earth is two, four, six, eight, and ten. The numbers one, three, five, seven, and nine are yang in nature. They add up to twenty-five. The numbers two, four, six, eight, and ten are yin in nature. They add up to thirty. The water of the kidneys is the numeric one. The one of water is followed by the two of fire, three of wood, four of metal, and five of earth. In these numerics of creation, three are yang and two are yin. The water of the kidneys is also the numeric six. The six of water is followed by the seven of fire, eight of wood, nine of metal, and ten of earth. In these numerics of completion, three are yin and two are yang.

"In the human body, the five elements also follow the rules of creation and completion. The kidneys belong to the element water; thus its numerics are one and six. The heart belongs to the element fire; thus its numerics are two and seven. The liver belongs to the element wood; thus it numerics are three and eight. The lungs belong to the element metal; thus its numerics are four and nine. The spleen belongs to the element earth; thus its numerics are five and ten. The viscera also have their yin and yang components. Yin reaches its limit in the numeric eight and is strongest in two. Therefore, when the vapor reaches the liver, the residual yin is purged from the kidneys, and when the vapor reaches the heart, the Great Ultimate will give birth to yin. The numeric two resides in the heart and the numeric eight resides in the liver. Yang is at the end of its limit in the numeric nine and is strongest in one. Therefore, when the fluid reaches the lungs, the residual yang is purged from the heart, and when the fluid reaches the kidneys, the Great Ultimate will give birth to yang. The numeric one resides in the kidneys and the numeric nine resides in the lungs. When practitioners can get the dragon and the tiger to copulate and gather the one true vapor of the heart, they are said to be gathering the numeric seven. When the numeric seven moves from the middle tan-t'ien to the lower tan-t'ien, the immortal fetus will be nourished. From the lower tan-t'ien, the numeric seven completes its course by returning to the heart. This process is called 'the numeric seven returning to the elixir field.'

"Yin wanes in the numerics two and eight. When the true vapor emerges, the numeric two will be purged and there will be no more yin in the heart. When the great medicine materializes, the numeric eight will be purged and there will no more yin in the liver. When the yin in the two and eight is purged, the yang of three and nine will grow. In this way yin will be purged from the liver and the heart will be strengthened. If the numeric three of the liver is strong, yang will be strong. After the numeric seven has returned to the heart to purge the fluid of the lungs, the numeric nine of the lungs will circulate and strengthen the heart. When the numeric nine of the lungs is strong, yang will be strong. When yang is strong, the yang of the numerics three and nine will grow. This process is called 'the numeric nine circulating and returning to the elixir field.' "

Lü said:

"In the Return of the numeric seven, the yang in the heart is returned to the heart to reside in the middle tan-t'ien. In the Circulation and Return of the numeric nine, the yang in the lungs, which originated from the heart, is also returned to the heart to reside in the middle tan-t'ien. Now that I know about the Return of the numeric seven and the Circulation and Return of the numeric nine, may I learn about the meaning of the upward and downward interaction of the golden and jade elixirs, the flow and ebb of yin and yang, and their return to the tan-t'iens?"

Chung said:

"In the past some people have argued that the 'return of the golden elixir' refers to the descent of the fluid of the lungs to the lower tan-t'ien. They have also said that the 'return of the jade elixir' is the descent of the fluid of the heart to the lower tan-t'ien. They are wrong. These statements don't even come close to describing the mysterious workings of heaven.

"Although the lungs give birth to the kidneys when metal creates water, it is incorrect to describe metal entering water as 'returning to the tan-t'ien.' Although the kidneys control the heart when water tames fire, it is incorrect to describe water entering fire as 'returning to the tan-t'ien.'

"The golden elixir is the fluid of the lungs, and this fluid encloses the immortal fetus. Together with the dragon and the tiger, the fluid and the fetus are escorted into the Yellow Chamber. When the great medicine is complete and extracting and replenishing have occurred behind the navel, the fluid of the lungs will fly up to the Upper Palace and then return to the middle tan-t'ien. *This* is the process of 'the golden elixir returning the tan-t'ien.'

"The jade elixir is the fluid of the kidneys. The fluid of the kidneys follows the upward movement of the primordial vapor and rises to gather at the heart. If you accumulate it, it will become the Golden Water. If you channel it upward, the Jade Pool will be filled. If you refine it, it will be transformed into White Snow. If you move it out of the middle tan-t'ien into the lower tan-t'ien, the immortal fetus will be bathed and steamed, provided that you have already collected the medicine. If you let it rise from the middle tan-t'ien and then direct it to the four limbs, the body will be refined and your bones will be purged of mundane dust. However, if it is not received [in the lower tan-t'ien], it will not rise. This cycle occurs endlessly and it is called 'the jade elixir returning to the tan-t'ien.'

"When yin reaches its limit, yang will be born. Within yang is the one true water. When this water rises with the yang, it is referred to as 'the yin returning to the field of yang.' When yang reaches its limit, yin will be born. Within yin is the one true vapor of yang. When this vapor descends with the yin, it is referred to as 'the yang returning to the field of yin.' In the process of repairing the brain and refining the top of the head, the lower returns to the upper. In the process of moistening and watering, the upper returns to the middle. In the process of cooking the pill and applying the fire, the upper returns to the lower. In the process of refining the form and heating the body, the lower returns to the middle.

"When the five elements interact in their reverse order, the three tan-t'iens will be tossed. As a result, the three fields will exchange contents with each other. This process will occur until the body is refined and transmuted into vapor and vapor is refined and transmuted into spirit. The spirit is first transported from the lower tan-t'ien to the middle tan-t'ien. Then it is moved from the middle to the upper tan-t'ien. Finally it is transported from the upper tan-t'ien to the Celestial Gate, where it will exit the body. At this time the mundane form will be left behind as the spirit enters the realm of the sacred. When the three transportations from the bottom to the top are complete, there will be no more 'returns.' "

14

Refining the Body

Lü asked:

"Now that I have learned about 'returning to the elixir fields,' can you tell me about the meaning of 'refining the body'?"

Chung said:

"When we are born, body and spirit are intertwined. The spirit is the ruler of the body and the body is the house of the spirit. Generative essence in the body gives birth to vapor and vapor gives birth to spirit. Fluid and vapor mutually create each other, forming the mother and the son in the body. Water gives birth to wood, wood to fire, fire to earth, earth to metal, and metal to water. The action of vapor follows the mother-son relationship and the flow of the fluid follows the husband-wife relationship. Such are the manifestations of yin and yang in the body.

"When yin receives yang, yin is born. Water is transformed into fluid, fluid is transformed into blood, and blood is transformed into saliva. However, if yin and yang do not interact properly, yin will not be born. As a result, mucus, tears, phlegm, and sweat will frequently flow out of the body. When yang receives yin, yang will be complete. Vapor is transmuted into generative essence, generative essence is transmuted into pearls, the pearls are transmuted into mercury, and mercury is transmuted into cinnabar grains. However, if yin and yang do not interact properly, yang will not be completed. As a result, we will age, become ill, suffer, and die.

"It is unthinkable that those who follow the Tao would cultivate yang but neglect yin. It is equally unbelievable that they would refine the self but forget about the substantive body. When the primordial vapor first enters the embryo, the vapors of our father and mother are at rest. Generative essence and blood enclose the fetus, and the entire bundle is stored inside the mother's place of pure yin. When yin is born within yin, a body will create another body. Even when the fetus is mature and is filled with vapor, it is still yin in nature. Even if it grows to six feet tall, it has within it only one spark of primordial yang. If you want to cultivate longevity, you must first refine the body so that you can survive the kalpas [karmic catastrophes] in the earthly realm. If you want to transcend the mundane and enter the sacred, you must refine the body and transmute it into vapor and then use your own body to create another body."

Lü said:

"The body is a manifestation of yin. Therefore yin has a form. Using form to attain the formless, we can transmute the body into vapor. In this way the mundane body is transformed into the sacred body. You say that this is the highest method of refining the body. First we use the body to retain the vapor; then we use the vapor to nourish it. Even if we manage to reap only small benefits from our cultivation, we will be able to live a healthy and long life. However, if we can reap large benefits, we will be able to retain our bodily form forever in the earthly realm. The old will become young and the young can maintain their youth and live a long life.

"There are three hundred sixty years in one great life cycle, thirty-six thousand years in one kalpa, and thirty-six thousand kalpas in one great kalpa. However, no one knows when the great kalpa will occur. Therefore, to be able to last as long as the sky and the earth and survive the kalpas, we must learn how to refine and preserve the body. Can you tell me how the body can be refined, how the transmutations are accomplished, and what the effects are?"

Chung said:

"In three hundred days the fetus will mature and the body will be developed completely. After birth the vapor will fill the body. The average height of a person is five feet five inches [Chinese measurement]: it is patterned after the numerics of the creation and completion of the five elements. Some are taller and some are shorter, but in general, people do not vary much from this measurement. The region above the heart is called the nine heavens and the region below the kidneys is called the nine earths. The distance between the kidneys and the heart is eight and four-tenths inches. Between the heart and the first level of the pagoda, the distance is again eight and four-tenths inches, and between the first level of the pagoda and the top of the head, the distance is also eight and four-tenths inches. From the kidneys to the crown of the head, the distance is two feet five and two-tenths inches. The primordial vapor reaches its maximum flow once every twenty-four hours [one day and one night] and travels a circuit of three hundred twenty measures. Each measure is equivalent to two feet five and two-tenths inches. Adding up to eighty-one [Chinese] cubits of primordial yang, the circuit is patterned exactly after the pure yang numeric of nine multiplied by nine. The distance between the heart and the kidneys is patterned after the structure of the sky and the earth. The distance from the kidneys to the crown of the head is two feet five inches and is patterned after the numerics of the five elements and the pure yang numeric of five multiplied by five.

"Primordial vapor is exhaled with exhalation. When it is exhaled, it will move unhindered to guard the body. The true vapor of the sky and the earth moves with the seasons and the changes in the weather. Moving to and from each other, they follow definite distances. The true vapor is inhaled with inhalation. When it enters the body, the meridians and the vessel pathways will be open. In one cycle of exhalation and inhalation, the true vapor of the sky, earth, and humanity will flow in and out of the twelve-story pagoda. Together, one inhalation and one exhalation are called one breath. During the period of one day and one night, there are thirteen thousand five hundred exhalations and thirteen thousand five hundred inhalations. That which is exhaled is our own primordial vapor and that which is inhaled is the true vapor of the sky and the earth. When the vapors of the sky and the earth flow into our body, the foundation of our root and source will be strengthened, and when the root is strong, the primordial vapor of the body will not dissipate. In one breath the true vapor of the sky and the earth can be absorbed to refine our vapor and be directed to the four directions in the body. When what is pure is strong, impurities will disappear and the circulation will flow unhindered. Vertically the vapor will thrust through the meridians; horizontally it will penetrate the vessel pathways. When this occurs, the body will feel invigorated and will not be harmed by heat or cold, or injured by labor. The bones will be strong, the body will feel light and unencumbered, and the breath will be pure and fresh. The true vapor is capable of keeping us young and healthy and can add years to our lives. However, if the foundation of our root and source is not strong, above, the primordial vapor will dissipate, and below, the palace of the origin cannot be repaired. The vapor we inhale from the sky and the earth will leak out of the body as soon as it enters. Eighty-one cubits of primordial vapor, as well as the numeric of nine multiplied by nine, will be lost. The vapor will not be ours to keep; instead it will be taken back by the sky and the earth. If we cannot capture the true vapor of the sky and the earth and keep it within, with time yin will accumulate and yang will decay. When the vapor within us is weak, we will get sick. When the vapor is completely dissipated, we will die and sink into countless cycles of reincarnation."

Lü asked:

"How can we prevent the vapor of primordial yang from leaking out so that we can use it to refine our body? How can we capture the true vapor of the sky and the earth so that we can survive the kalpas?"

Chung said:

"If you want to win a battle, you will need a strong army. If you want the people to be contented, the nation must be wealthy. In the body the primordial vapor is the army. When it stands guard inside, it will rid the body of yin; when it moves out, it will capture the true vapor of the sky and the earth. The body is like a country. If the country is rich, every citizen will be fed. Like a country, if the body is strong, it will lack nothing. Even if all the doors are open, nothing will be lost. If the circulation is unhindered, the body will be replenished mysteriously. When the circulation moves between the front and the back, form will be refined and heat will engulf the body. When it moves up and down, vapor will nurture the yang and purge the yin. Ch'ien and k'un will be heated according to schedule, and vapor and fluid will be tempered daily. When the jade elixir is used to refine the body, the dragon of the east will rise and White Snow will be seen fluttering around the mundane shell. When the golden elixir and the jade elixir are used to refine the body, the Thunder Wheel will descend and a golden light will float around in your meditation chamber."

Lü asked:

"Now that I have a little understanding of how the body can be refined, can you tell me more about the golden elixir and the jade elixir?"

Chung said:

"If the golden elixir is used to refine the body, the bones will turn gold, the body will radiate a golden light, and golden flower petals will be seen floating in the air. These are signs that the five vapors have moved toward the primordial regions and the three yangs have gathered on top of the head. It is the day that you will transcend the mundane body and complete the Great Golden Pill. If the jade elixir is used to refine the body, the skin and muscles will be moist with the Milk of the Sun and the body will glow like the jade tree. The Red Wine and the Jade Medicine will transform the mundane body, bright rays will shoot into your shell, and flowers will fly around as if swirled by a gentle wind. These are signs that the body has been transformed into vapor.

"Although many are familiar with the methods of 'returning to the elixir fields,' few know about the techniques of refining the body. When the jade elixir has returned to the tan-t'iens, it will bathe the immortal fetus and send it upward. At this time you must use the Waterwheel to drive it to the four directions. First, when the liver receives it, light will fill the eyes and the pupils will be bright and clear. Second, when the heart receives it, the mouth will generate the numinous fluid and the fluid will become the White Snow. Third, when the spleen receives it, the skin will take on a rosy hue and all scars will disappear. Fourth, when the lungs receive it, a fragrant scent will accompany the body and the complexion will resemble that of a child. Lastly, when the kidneys receive it, the elixir will have returned to its original home. You will hear the music of pipes and your hair will turn from white to black. These are the results of using the jade elixir to refine the body.

"If you want to use the golden elixir to refine the body, you must apply it when the process of the 'return to the tan-t'ien' has just begun but is not completed. When the golden elixir meets the ruling fire, the two will temper each other. After the golden elixir has returned to the tan-t'ien, it will rise again to battle with the true yin. This process is called 'refining the substantive body.'

"Originally earth tames water. However, if the golden elixir is in the earth, its light will be reflected back to the Yellow Emperor in the center and it will be united with the great yin. Originally fire tames metal. However, if the golden elixir is in the fire, the red seed will be merged with the furnace and the purple vapor will be born.

"When fire emerges from water, the yin in the yang will disappear and the golden pill will crystallize in the Yellow Chamber. When the yang spirit is tempered in the five vapors, green vapor will thrust up from the liver, white vapor will emerge in the lungs, red vapor will appear in the heart, black vapor will rise in the kidneys, and yellow vapor will settle in the spleen. All five vapors will move toward the central region, where, following the ruling fire, they will penetrate and enter the Inner Court. In the lower region, yin will disappear in the yang within the yin and yang will rise to gather in the palace of the spirit. In the central region, the yang within the yang will be pure and will rise to gather in the palace of the spirit. In the Yellow Chamber, the great medicine will be purely yang and will rise to gather in the palace of the spirit. The five fluids will move toward the lower region, the five vapors will move toward the central region, and the five yangs will move toward the upper region. After the three gatherings are complete and after three thousand merits have been accumulated, the crane will dance at the top of the head and the dragon will leap up inside the body. You will hear sweet music and see falling flowers. The foundations of the Purple Chamber will be complete and the true fragrance will float around you. After you have accumulated three thousand more merits, you will leave the dust of the world and will no longer live among mortals. When the stick of incense is extinguished, you will become a resident of the lands of immortality. Transcending the mundane, you will shed your shell, enter the realm of the sacred, and become an immortal."

15

Moving to the Primordial Regions

Lü asked:

"Now that I know about the principles of refining the body, can you tell me the meaning of 'moving to the primordial regions'?"

Chung said:

"When the great medicine is realized, the jade elixir will return to the tan-t'iens to bathe the immortal fetus. When the true vapor emerges, it will thrust the jade elixir upward to transform the bones of the mundane body. This process is called 'using the jade elixir to refine the body.' When the golden sparks fly out from behind the navel, the Waterwheel will transport them into the Inner Court. Moving from the top to the middle and then from the middle to the lower region, the golden elixir will return to the tan-t'iens to cultivate the golden cinnabar. When the five vapors move toward the primordial centers, the three yangs will gather at the top of the head and the vapor will be refined into spirit. However, the movement of the five vapors to the primordial regions does not only refine the body and allow us to live forever in the earthly realm. The meaning of 'moving to the primordial regions' is known only to a few. Sages past and present are reluctant to talk about it because this method of realizing immortality is hidden deep in the workings of the sky and the earth. It is the highest secret of the three pure realms: its mysterious principles cannot be described and its subtleties cannot be asked about or explained. The sages were afraid that the students would be unable to grasp the meaning and would be too confused to ask the right questions. Thus, in the past, the teachers of the Tao were unwilling to reveal the sacred workings of the Tao, afraid that if they did, they would harm themselves as well as others."

Lü said:

"First we must understand the Tao and the meaning of immortality. Next we need to learn to apply the alchemical schedules and penetrate the workings of heaven. Then we need to recognize the true sources of water and fire, realize that the dragon and the tiger are not born in the liver and the lungs, be familiar with the all-important principle of extracting and replenishing, and understand that lead and mercury are not k'an and li.

"You have taught me the method of reversing the cycle of the five elements and have described to me the tossing of the three tan-t'iens. I am now familiar with the principles of 'returning to the tan-t'iens' and 'refining the body.' I know deeply about the techniques of cultivating longevity and I understand the principles of transcending the mundane and entering the sacred. And now I also realize that the method by which we can ascend to immortality is built on refining the vapor and moving it to the primordial regions. Can you tell me what is meant by 'moving to the primordial regions'?"

Chung said:

"The Tao has no form. The great source is originally simple. The clear on top and the muddy at the bottom are merged into one undifferentiated whole. When the great simplicity divided, the primal beginning emerged from the one undifferentiated whole to become sky and earth. Within the sky and the earth, the five directions east, west, south, north, and center are born. Each direction has a ruling emperor, and each emperor has two children—one yang and one yin. These children are the two vapors. The two vapors mutually create and complete each other to give birth to the five elements. The five elements mutually create and complete each other to give birth to the six weather patterns, which are called the three yins and the three yangs.

"Humans are conceived in the same way as the universe was created. When the fetus is first conceived, generative essence and vapor are merged. Then essence and vapor separate to form the two kidneys. The kidney on the left is called the 'mystery,' and the 'mystery' ascends with the vapor to be transported into the liver. The kidney on the right is called the 'female,' and the female follows the path of the fluid down to the bladder. The 'mysterious female' originally came from nothingness; it is from nothingness that all things are generated. Coming from the true vapor of our father and mother, the mysterious female is rooted in the ground of pure yin. Therefore it is said that the valley spirit that does not die is called the mysterious female. The entrance to the mysterious female is the root of the sky and the earth. The mysterious female is the two kidneys. It is from the kidneys that the five viscera and the six organs are created. The liver belongs to the element wood; it is called chia and i, and it is analogous to the green emperor of the east. The heart belongs to the element fire; it is called ping and ting, and it is analogous to the red emperor of the south. The lungs belong to the element metal; they are called keng and hsin, and they are analogous to the white emperor of the west. The spleen belongs to the element earth; it is called wu and chi, and it is analogous to the yellow emperor of the center. The kidneys belong to the element water; they are called jen and kuei, and they are analogous to the black emperor of the north.

"At the time of conception, there is neither form nor shape; there is only one yin and one yang. When the fetus is mature, the intestines and stomach are formed. The six vapors are separated into three males and three females. The one undifferentiated vapor controls the five elements and the five elements control the six vapors. First to emerge are yin and yang, the yang within the yin, and the yin within the yang. Next to emerge are metal, wood, water, fire, and earth. Within the five elements, there are also the fire within the water, the water within the fire, the metal within the water, the wood within the metal, the fire within the wood, and the earth within the fire. When the five elements interact, the yin and yang vapors are separated into six vapors. Thus the Great Tao creates the five elements through differentiation.

"After the winter solstice the first ray of yang appears in the land. As it spreads to the five directions, yang will be born. One emperor rules each season, assisted by the other four. If the black emperor does not relinquish his rule in spring, cold will not be transformed into warmth; and if the red emperor is not prepared to take over in summer, warmth will not be transformed into heat. After the summer solstice the one ray of yin is born in the land. As it spreads to the five directions, yin will descend. Again, one emperor rules, assisted by the other four. If the red emperor does not relinquish his rule in autumn, heat will not be transformed into coolness; and if the black emperor is not prepared to take over in winter, coolness will not be transformed into cold. After the winter solstice, yang is born in the earth and its vapor moves toward the sky. After the summer solstice, yin is born in the sky and its vapor moves toward the earth. Those who follow the Tao must understand thoroughly the meaning of these things. Within each day and month, when the first ray of yang is born, the vapors of the five viscera will move toward the central primordial region. When the first ray of yin is born, the fluids of the five viscera will move toward the lower primordial region. When the yang within the yin, the yang within the yang, and the yang within the yin and yang all move toward the upper region, the spirit of the mind in the Internal Court will return to the Celestial Palace. This is what is meant by 'moving toward the primordial regions.'"

Lü said:

"When yang is born, the five vapors will move toward the central primordial region. When yin is born, the five fluids will move toward the lower primordial region. In addition, the yang within the yang, the yang within the yin, and the yang within the yin and yang will move toward the upper primordial region. Serious practitioners have heard about these processes, but no one knows how they can liberate us from the dust of the world."

Chung said:

"When yang is born, the vapor of primordial yang will move toward the central primordial region. This is natural. When yin is born, fluid created from the accumulation of vapor will move toward the lower primordial region. This is also natural. If you follow the methods and practice diligently, you will be liberated from the dust of the world. However, if you want to transcend the mundane, enter the sacred, shed your shell, and become an immortal, you must first get the dragon and the tiger to copulate. Then you must create the great medicine. Once the great medicine is realized, the true vapor will emerge. When the true vapor emerges, first you must apply the monthly schedule yearly, using the lunar calendar to determine the phases of flow and ebb. Then you must apply the daily schedule monthly, following the appropriate ruling numerics. Lastly you must apply the hourly schedule daily, following the correct numerics of the cycle of inhalation and exhalation. If you use yang to nurture yang, the yin residue will be purged from the yang, and if you use yang to refine yin, the yang will not dissipate from the yin.

"In spring the liver is strong and the spleen is weak. In summer the heart is strong and the lungs are weak. In autumn the lungs are strong and the liver is weak. In winter the kidneys are strong and the heart is weak. The kidneys are the root and foundation of life. In each of the four seasons, there are three weeks in which the spleen is strong and the kidneys are weak. Thus the kidneys are injured in all four seasons. This is why many people get sick easily.

"When chia and i rule in the liver, we need to guard against blockage of circulation in the spleen. When ping and ting rule in the heart, we need to guard against blockage of circulation in the lungs. When wu and chi rule in the spleen, we need to guard against blockage of circulation in the kidneys. When keng and hsin rule in the lungs, we need to guard against blockage of circulation in the liver. When jen and kuei rule in the kidneys, we need to guard against blockage of circulation in the heart. When the vapor of one organ is full, the vapors of the others are at ebb, and when one of the viscera is strong, the others are weak. This is also another reason why many people are unhealthy.

"The vapor of the heart germinates in the hour of hai [9:00–11:00 P.M.] and is born in the hour of yin [3:00–5:00 A.M.]; it waxes strong in the hour of ssu [9:00–11:00 A.M.] and is weak in the hour of shen [3:00–5:00 P.M.]. The vapor of the liver germinates in shen and is born in hai; it waxes strong in yin and is weak in ssu. The vapor of the lungs germinates in yin and is born in ssu; it waxes strong in shen and is weak in hai. The vapor of the kidneys germinates in ssu and is born in shen; it waxes strong in hai and is weak in yin. In spring the vapor of the spleen follows the behavior of the vapor of the liver, in summer it follows that of the heart, in autumn that of the lungs, and in winter that of the kidneys. People nowadays know nothing about the daily schedule and are unfamiliar with the hours of waxing and waning. Therefore they get ill easily.

"During specific times in the year, month, and hour, the three yangs are gathered. When this occurs, you should refine the yang and prevent yin from emerging. During specific times in the year, month, and hour, the three yins will accumulate. When this occurs, you should nurture the yang and prevent it from dissipating. The true vapor that is born inside you is the vapor of pure yang. Therefore it is important that you refine the vapors of the five viscera, still the breath, and direct the vapors up to the Celestial Pool. When you have accomplished all this, first the yin in the kidneys will disappear and the waters of the Nine Rivers will be still. Second, the yin in the liver will disappear and the eight gates will be shut. Third, the yin will disappear in the lungs and metal and fire will be brought together in the furnace. Fourth, the yin will disappear from the spleen and the Jade Chamber will be sealed. Finally, the true vapor will rise and the four vapors will merge as one. Even if the golden fluid tries to descend, this little cup of liquid will not be able to oppose the full force of the fire. As a result, fire will enclose water and the two will unite and enter the palace of the spirit. When this happens, you should slow the breath and turn your gaze inward. When the one intention does not stray, the spirit will become omniscient. In stillness you will hear music and songs. You will feel as if you are in a dream, but you are actually not dreaming. Rather, you are immersed in emptiness. The environment that you experience will be completely different from that of mundane existence. Nothing in this world can equal its splendor: the buildings are like palaces, the roofs are covered with sparkling green tiles, the trellises shine like pearls, and the air is thick with fragrance. These are signs that the yang spirit has left the Inner Court to return to the upper tan-t'ien. When the spirit is refined further, it will be lifted to immortality to merge with the Great Tao. When the spirit thrusts through the Celestial Gate, the subtle body will be bathed in a golden glow. Flowers will land on the mundane body and swirl through the air like ripples in water. One movement of an arm or a leg will send you traveling ten thousand miles. If the yang spirit is returned to the shell, spirit and body will merge and you will be able to live as long as the sky and the earth. At this point you can choose to live forever in the earthly realm or leave the mundane shell and return to the ten continents. If you choose to leave, you will be carried to the purple palace of the emperor Tzu-wei, where you will be escorted to your original home. Your name and the merits that you have accumulated will be entered in the register, you will be allowed to live and wander in the three islands, and you will be liberated from the confines of earthly wind and dust. This is what is meant by 'being liberated from the dust and transcending the mundane.'"

16

Internal Observation

Lü asked:
"What is 'internal observation'?"
Chung said:
"The methods of internal observation [forgetting oneself] and visualization have been used by some practitioners and not by others.

"The scheming mind is like a monkey and the will is like a horse: they run wild and cannot stop. In order to prevent attachments and desires from destroying our motivation to cultivate [the Tao], the sages have recommended that we use visual images to block our ears and eyes to temptations, so that our minds will not be wayward and our intention will not be distracted. In this respect the methods of visualization and internal observation [forgetting oneself] are very useful. However, many practitioners do not understand the real function of these techniques. Not knowing when yin and yang interact and ignorant of the methods of applying fire, they think that visualization alone will help them succeed in their cultivation. Believing that they can realize the pill by directing their intention, they form images of collecting the medicine. They inhale rigorously and swallow saliva; they gaze at the sun and the moon in the sky; and they talk about the principles of nonaction found in the sky and the earth. They focus on the mouth and the belly, not knowing that this is but child's play.

"The few who have successfully used the methods of visualization and forgetting oneself know that treasures that are gathered in dreams are useless, because dreams vanish in the morning. They also understand that dreaming of cakes will not satisfy hunger. If you practice the methods incorrectly, you are only building empty wishes on illusions. Like flowers in a mirror and the reflection of the moon in water, your cultivation will not have any substance. Even if you practice diligently, you will achieve nothing.

"If you want to use the methods of visualization and forgetting oneself, you must understand that the mind is stirred easily and that it is difficult to subdue the will. You must know that these methods should be used only at the appointed time and under appropriate conditions. It is not enough to find a secluded place and sit quietly. The mind is easily led astray by things in the world, and the will is easily influenced by emotions. If you do not follow the correct procedures, you will be as far from success as the distance between the sky and the earth. Even if you practice for months and years, you will not get results. If the mind is confused and the will is wild, your efforts will come to nothing. If you are too focused on visual images, you will see only the beauty of the green elixir and will never notice its radiance. If you are too intent on listening to the sound of flutes, you will never notice the roar of the thunder. The senses play only a small role in the method of visualization. Even if you travel and search the six directions, you are not guaranteed to find the right method. And if you do not have the correct method, how can you use visualization and internal observation to help your cultivation?"

Lü asked:

"Can you tell me briefly how to practice visualization and internal observation?"

Chung said:

"For example, to facilitate the rise of yang, you should visualize the following images: male, dragon, fire, sky, clouds, crane, the sun, horse, smoke, haze, the wheel, horse cart, flowers, and steam. All these images are associated with the rise of yang. To facilitate the descent of yin, you should visualize the following images: female, tiger, water, earth, rain, tortoise, the moon, oxen, spring, mud, lead, and leaves. All these images are associated with the descent of yin.

"The green dragon, the white tiger, the red raven, the black tortoise, the five mountains, the nine continents, the four seas, the three islands, the golden boy and jade lady, the Waterwheel, and the pagoda are all useful visual images. You can also use the names of various processes of cultivation to evoke visual images. However, if you visualize images only for the purpose of stilling the spirit, you will be no different from a fisherman who loses the basket before catching the fish and a hunter who lets the hare escape before capturing it. To move the postcelestial wheel, you must have the prototype of the precelestial wheel, and to complete the great vessel, you must have the pattern of the lesser vessel. The methods of internal observation and visualization do not tolerate mistakes. You cannot use them indefinitely and you cannot treat them as the ultimate technique. When all thinking stops, this is true cognition. True cognition means true emptiness, and true emptiness occurs when you are no longer imprisoned by ignorance. Only when you are close to the final liberation, only after the foundations are completed, and only after you have begun to apply the daily schedule should you use the method of visualization to assist your practice. However, as the days toward your union with the Tao grow fewer, and as you enter the state of the intangible, you should practice visualization less and less and should begin to use the method of internal observation."

Lü asked:

"What should we visualize to facilitate the copulation of the dragon and the tiger and the coupling of yin and yang?"

Chung said:

"When yin and yang interact to anchor k'an and li, this is what you should visualize: You should form the image of the nine true immortal kings rising up, leading a boy dressed in red. Simultaneously, you should also form the image of the nine true queen mothers descending, leading a girl dressed in white. The boy and the girl meet in front of the yellow house, where they are welcomed by an old woman dressed in yellow. Feel their bliss and pleasure as they lie with their sexual companion. Then visualize the girl continuing to descend and the boy continuing to rise. Like lovers separating, they part and go their own ways. When this episode finishes, you should visualize the old woman in yellow carrying a bundle shaped like a red orange. She throws the bundle into the yellow house, where it is held in a golden container. The boy is ch'ien looking for k'un. When yang returns to its position, it will carry the yin with it back to its home. The girl is k'un searching for ch'ien. When yin returns to its position, it will carry the yang with it back to its home. These are the visual images associated with the interaction of k'an and li and the coupling of yin and yang.

"The following visualizations will facilitate the formation of the yellow sprouts. First, visualize a black tiger leaping up in the fiery flames and a red dragon descending into the stormy sea. The two animals meet and battle in front of the terrace of the pagoda. The red gate opens wide, and a majestic being appears in the roaring flames and foaming seas to direct the great fires to heat the sky. Above, giant waves rise and fall. The fires also rise and then fall, filling the air with smoke. The dragon and the tiger swirl around each other and then enter the golden container. Below, the yellow house is enclosed inside a steamer. These are the visual images associated with the copulation of the dragon and the tiger and their transformation into the yellow sprouts."

Lü asked:

"Now that I know about the visualizations associated with the coupling of yin and yang and the copulation of the dragon and the tiger, may I hear about the visualizations associated with stoking the fire, heating the pill, and refining the medicine?"

Chung said:

"Visualize a container shaped like a cauldron or a crucible. It is round like a wheel and its color can be yellow or black. On its left is a green dragon and on its right is a white tiger. In front is a red raven and at the back is a black tortoise. Accompanying it on both sides are two ministers dressed in purple robes. They bow and then stand attentively. Behind them are servants and assistants. When the fire is ignited under the container, a prince in a red robe appears. He rides a red horse and descends through a red cloud. He is waving a whip, and pointing at the flames, he tells you that the fires are not strong enough. The flames leap higher as they try to shoot up to the sky. However, the Celestial Gate is closed. The fires now surge downward and spread to all directions. The people, the crucible, the prince, and the ministers are now all engulfed in the red flames, all shouting and telling you to increase the heat of the fire. The water in the container begins to bubble, although vapor cannot be seen. The pearl within the water glows, although it is not bright. These are the visual images associated with stoking the fire, heating the pill, and refining the medicine."

Lü said:

"The visualizations do not end at gathering the medicine and stoking the fire. I take it that the subsequent processes of internal transformations can also be facilitated by visualizations."

Chung said:

"Visualize thunder clouds descending and the smoke of fires rising, or flowers falling like rain, or a gentle breeze and a caressing wind emerging from the chamber of the palace. Or, visualize female immortals on multicolored phoenixes appearing through the green haze. Then visualize these women offering a golden bowl filled with jade dew or a thick cloudy liquid to the prince down below. These images can all be used to facilitate the return of the golden elixir to the tan-t'iens.

"Next, visualize the dragon, the tiger, and the Waterwheel immersed in fire and rushing to penetrate the three gates. Each gate is guarded by many armed and fierce soldiers. The dragon and the tiger alone cannot break through, but the gates open when strong fires are applied. The K'un-lun Mountains are penetrated, and the Waterwheel continues to move upward until it reaches the Celestial Pool. Then visualize three cranes flying up to the sky, or a pair of butterflies entering the three palaces, or the little boy in red being carried through the Celestial Gate on five-colored clouds, or the prince being transported to the three realms in a jade carriage with golden wheels. These images can all be used to facilitate the ejection of the golden sparks from behind the navel and the movement of the Great Waterwheel.

"Then visualize the red-robed ambassador in the chariot touring the continents: from the continent of i to ching, from ching to ch'ing, from ch'ing to hsü, from hsü to yang, from yang to ching [different from the previous ching], from ching to liang, from liang to yung, and from yung back to li. After moving to the east, west, south, and north, the chariot rests at the continent of yü. From there the circulation begins again. Having obtained the gold and the jade, ch'ien has completed its tasks. The leader issues an order and the nine continents are linked. The circulation now moves without obstruction. It can travel to the five mountains, beginning at Mount Heng, or it can cross the five lakes, starting at the North Lake. Carrying the celestial decrees, it can command the five emperors and summon the five dukes. These images can all be used to facilitate the 'return to the tan-t'iens.'

"Next visualize pieces of sparkling jade falling to the ground, or rain and dew showering the earth, or waves rolling from the sea to fill the hundred rivers, or the sun helping seeds to germinate, or fire engulfing the land, or smoke and mist enveloping the universe. These images can all be used to facilitate the process of refining the body.

"Finally, visualize the crane leaving its nest, or the dragon exiting its lair, or the five emperors gazing at the sky, or the five-colored clouds rising, or the red phoenix flying through raindrops of jade, or your dreaming body flying up to the celestial heights, or flower petals falling around wildly. Think about celestial music filling the air, visualize a golden light enveloping your body, and imagine yourself entering the palace of splendors. These images can all be used to facilitate the process of 'moving toward the primordial regions.' Once you get to this point of your cultivation, you should abandon the method of visualization and switch to the method of internal observation."

Lü said:

"The principles of internal observation are different from those of visualization. Can you elaborate on them?"

Chung said:

"Many practitioners do not understand the workings of heaven and do not know how to use internal observation to facilitate cultivation. Wanting to achieve liberation quickly, they believe that fetal breathing is simply inhaling more and exhaling less. They think that internal observation simply means closing their eyes and stopping the thoughts. Little do they know that this kind of stillness can only liberate the yin spirit. Thus, at best they can only become a ghost with a pure spirit; they can never become an immortal of pure yang. The sages and immortals have told us to gather the medicine, apply the fires, extract lead to replenish mercury, return the elixir to the tan-t'iens, refine the body, move toward the three primordial regions, and merge with the vapor. Afraid that practitioners would not understand these principles, they spoke about these methods in detail. However, they did not say much about internal observation.

"The method of internal observation is a technique that allows us to exchange yin for yang, and it should be practiced only when we are ready to leave the mundane and be transformed into an immortal. Do not belittle this method, and make sure that you learn it well. Everything that I have said about the transition from mortal to immortal occurs at a specific time in the process of cultivation. If you understand the method of internal observation and trust it, and if you practice it correctly at the appropriate time, you will achieve the expected results.

"The practice of internal observation is not tied to specific times of the day and does not have specific procedures. When it is time for you to leave the mundane, you should find a quiet room, practice it day and night, learn to recognize the yang spirit, and be ready to drive away the yin ghosts. Bodhidharma faced the wall for nine years before he entered the Inner Court; the World-Honored One [Buddha] spent six years stilling his mind before he emerged from the confines of the mundane. From these examples you should know that internal observation is not easy to practice.

"When the circulation moves from above to below and when the Purple Waterwheel enters the Celestial Palace, you will see the riches of heaven floating in front of you. Things that you admire and wish for will appear and disappear, and things that are normally difficult to obtain will be given to you. Practitioners who have lived a simple life away from worldly luxuries will especially feel happy when they are presented with these splendid things at the completion of their cultivation. Surrounded by buildings covered with pearls and jade and in the midst of the music of reed pipes, good foods, exquisite plants, and breathtaking scenery, they will feel as if they are immersed in a beautiful painting. They do not know, however, that the celestial paradise they experience is only a reflection of the Inner Court inside the body. If you get attached to these images and feelings, you will be locked forever inside these illusions. Consequently, you will be stuck in the earthly realm and will not be able to liberate your shell and become an immortal. If you practice internal observation incorrectly, not only will you not enter the Celestial Palace, but you will conjure up yin ghosts and monsters. These unwholesome influences will in turn create a world of illusions called the Monster Wheel. If you are influenced by wayward thoughts, you will stray into evil ways and be enticed into practicing techniques that are not a part of the Tao. Not only will you not attain immortality, but you will be hounded by the three monsters and seven souls who want you dead. Forever chased by the nine worms and the six thieves who thrive on your suffering, you will have nowhere to run or hide."

17

Monsters and Obstacles

Lü said:

"Internal observation helps us to focus the spirit so that we can refine it and send it into the Inner Court. From there the spirit will thrust through the Celestial Gate and enter the realm of the sacred. Leaving the body, the spirit exits and reenters smoothly and faultlessly. Traveling far or hovering near, it knows the distance it is capable of journeying. If we wish to stay in the earthly realm, the spirit will merge with the body. If we want to ascend to immortality, the spirit will wander the Peng-lai Islands. If we practice the method of internal observation correctly, with time we will be able to transcend the mundane. However, if dark ghosts and monsters appear, how do we conquer them? And how can we be assured that we will eventually ascend to immortality?"

Chung said:

"Those who follow the Tao must first develop trust in the methods and not let fortune, fame, and desire cloud their goal. Then, having made their decision to cultivate [the Tao], they should stay with it. Practice diligently, live a simple life away from the clutter of material things, and do not stray from the beginner's mind. If you set your goal on great achievements, you will attain only moderate achievements, and if you set your goal on moderate achievements, you will attain only small achievements. If you do not understand the Great Tao, you will never know its secret workings. Consequently, you will be familiar with only the minor methods. Lost in untried procedures and strange techniques, you will waste your time and attain nothing. You will get old and die and be trapped in endless cycles of reincarnation. The failures of generations of practitioners have convinced many that longevity and liberation from the mundane world are just empty talk. Moreover, many hear about the Tao but do not understand it. Thus their minds are easily stirred by happenings in the world and their motivation is easily weakened by attachment to material things. In the end they are unable to escape from the ten monsters and the nine obstacles."

Lü asked:

"What are the nine obstacles?"

Chung said:

"Before the great medicine is completed, you will feel the cold and the heat and will need to change your clothes with the seasons. Before the true vapor is born, you will feel hunger and thirst, and every day you will want to eat three meals. Being hampered by the need for clothing and food—this is the first obstacle.

"When the burdens of karma are great, you will need to repay what you have owed in previous lifetimes. Oppressed by work, you will not have much time to practice. When you try to set aside time for your cultivation, your aging parents will make you feel guilty about abandoning them. Although you want to cultivate, you are unable to find the time. Being smothered by parental demands—this is the second obstacle.

"When you are attached to your family, you will worry about your spouse and your children. Daily your emotional attachment to them will grow. Driven to provide food and shelter for them, you work tirelessly day and night. Although your mind has a tendency toward stillness, you are hindered by the anxiety of daily life. Being bound by love and attach-ment—this is the third obstacle.

"When you are rich and powerful, you will find it difficult to give up material goods and fame. Not content with what you have, you will always want more. Being drowned by fame and fortune—this is the fourth obstacle.

"In your youth you were unwilling to cultivate, and in old age you continue to injure your spirit. Even when you lose your vitality and become ill, your mischievous mind still re-fuses to wake up. Or you were born into hardship and were doomed to suffer all your life. Being plagued by self-inflicted suffering and crushed by difficult livelihood—this is the fifth obstacle.

"When you are impatient to find a teacher, you will not care whether the teacher is enlightened or not. Impressed by what the teacher claims he can offer and falling prey to his charisma, you believe that you have found a true immortal. Eventually you discover too late that the teacher is a fraud who is after fame and power. Being fooled and controlled by false teachers—this is the sixth obstacle.

"When you listen to debates among teachers and fellow students, you are bound to be led astray by their suggestions. You search blindly through a tangle of leaves and branches and then discover that there is nothing worthwhile. These so-called teachers and their students are interested only in ar-guing about the relative merits of lesser techniques. They do not know that the sun and the moon do not rise easily, and that when they rise, the light is so brilliant that it can be seen by all. They do not know that the thunder does not roar trivi-ally, but when it does, the sound is so deafening that it can be heard by all. They try to dazzle each other with words, not realizing that their elegant speeches are like the fleeting lights of exploding fireworks. Bickering over semantics, they argue endlessly and can never agree on anything. Being blinded by discussions and arguments—this is the seventh obstacle.

"You decide to cultivate in the morning but change your

mind in the evening. When you try to meditate, you discover that you have lost your motivation. You put off your cultivation because there is always something else to do. You are enthusiastic in the beginning but lose your interest soon afterward. Being trapped by laziness and lack of motivation—this is the eighth obstacle.

"You waste away the years of your life, the months of the years, the days of the month, and the hours of the day. In your youth you are occupied with fame and fortune. In old age you are worried about children and grandchildren. Each year you wait for the next year and each day you wait for the next day. Refusing to believe that what you practice today will help you tomorrow, you complain in your old age that you cannot recapture your youth. Always waiting for the next month or the next year to cultivate—this is the ninth obstacle.

"Those who follow the Tao must understand that if they succumb to one or two of the nine obstacles, they will not be able to succeed in their cultivation, even if they practice diligently."

Lü asked:

"Now that I have heard about the nine obstacles, can you tell me about the ten monsters?"

Chung said:

"The practitioner can encounter the ten monsters in three situations: during waking life, in dreams, and while practicing internal observation.

"When you encounter images and sensations of many-colored flowers, the sound of reed flutes, sweet flavors in your mouth, fragrant scents, pleasure throughout the body, and general exhilaration and excitement, you should ignore them, because this is the monster called the six thieves.

"When you encounter images of beautiful chambers and terraces, exquisite decorative ornaments, silk curtains and window frames studded with pearls, rooms lined with tapestries, floors highlighted with coral beads, halls filled with gold and jade, you should ignore them, because this is the monster called wealth.

"When you encounter images of prize horses, finely decorated saddles, houses built like palaces, titles, thousands of acres of lands, gifts from diplomats, halls decorated with green and purple cloth, and richly embroidered shoes and boots, you should ignore them, because this is the monster called political power.

"When you encounter images and sensations of wispy clouds, lazy sunny afternoons, windstorms and heavy rain, thunder and lightning, the mournful music of flutes, and sounds of weeping, you should ignore them, because this is the monster called the six emotions.

"When you encounter images of family and relatives suffering from natural disasters, children falling ill, parents dying, siblings being separated, and spouses leaving each other, you should ignore them, because this is the monster called possessive love.

"When you encounter images and sensations of being burned by fire, falling off a cliff, being stung by swarms of insects, being poisoned, being robbed by bandits on the road, breaking the law and getting executed, you should ignore them, because this is the monster called personal catastrophe.

"When you encounter images of the ten terrestrial realms glowing with yang energy, the three pure realms, the Jade Emperor, the four guardians, the seven lights [of the Dipper], the five emperors, and the eight kings standing in ceremonial solemnity or floating around leisurely, you should ignore them, because this is the monster called sacred beings.

"When you encounter images and sensations of soldiers, sharp weapons, fierce war cries, bows and arrows aimed at you, and you have no place to hide, you should ignore them, because this is the monster called war.

"When you encounter images and sensations of rows of musicians in front of you, sounds of flutes and reed pipes, dancers moving around the room, costumes rustling past you, and a pair of lead dancers in red presenting you a platter piled with gold, you should ignore them, because this is the monster called seductive music.

"When you encounter images of beautiful companions wearing fine jewelry, drinks and food laid out on the terraces at night, sexy bodies in seductive clothing, soft whispers asking you to be a sexual companion, you should ignore them, because this is the monster called sexual desire.

"When you encounter the ten monsters, you should ignore them. If you attend to them, you will be attached to them, and if you are attached to them, you will be grasping at them. Many people fail to attain the Tao because they fall prey to the monsters. If you are not attracted to the monsters in waking life, you will be able to ignore them when you encounter them. Consequently, your mind will not wander and your motivation will not be shaken. If you are able to ignore the monsters in dreams, the mind will not stray and the spirit will not dissipate. If you encounter the monsters while you are practicing internal observation, you must dismiss them as illusions. Do not get swept up by the tide of your thoughts and emotions and do not treat them as though they are your sons. Burn the body with the three true fires and they will go away. Then use the Purple Waterwheel to carry the yang spirit through the Internal Court into the Celestial Palace. Only then can you attain transcendence.

"Many practitioners want to cultivate clarity and stillness but are unable to escape from the ten monsters and the nine obstacles. Slaves to the external environment, they are followers of the Tao only in name. They do not know how to cultivate in daily life, and they think that if they left the dust of the world and retreated to a remote place, they could attain the Tao. In actual fact, the nine obstacles and the ten monsters are with them all their lives.

"Even if you succumb to one or two of the ten monsters, you will not be able to attain the Tao. At best you will get moderate or small benefits from your cultivation and become an immortal among mortals or an earth immortal. However, if you can remove all the monsters and the obstacles and follow the procedures of cultivation correctly, each step of practice will bring you closer to immortality. Finally, if you use internal observation to unite your body with the yang spirit, you will not have to wait long to return to the three islands."

18

Experiences and Feedback

Lü said:

"Nobody wants to be ill; that's why the followers of the Tao aspire to live a healthy and peaceful life. Nobody wants to die; that's why the followers of the Tao cultivate to attain longevity. Mortals are tied to the realm of humanity, but the followers of the Tao are able to ascend to immortality and wander in other realms of existence. Mortals are confined to the earthly realm, but the followers of the Tao can eventually transcend the mundane world and enter the celestial caverns. Thus, those who cultivate the Tao are willing to undergo hardship, live simply, be free of worldly cares, and seclude themselves in remote places. Because they practice in isolation, they are often ignorant of their progress. Not knowing when they should begin the next stage of training, they risk making mistakes that can take a long time to correct. After practitioners begin their cultivation, how can they know that they are following the correct procedures?"

Chung said:

"If you are disciplined in your practice but do not get results, it is not the fault of the Tao. Rather, it is because you did not get instructions from an enlightened teacher. If you were taught incorrect methods and if you followed erroneous techniques, you will never get results. If you are ignorant of the schedule of the transformations, you will also fail in your cultivation. Again, this is not the fault of the Tao. If, on the other hand, you received correct instructions from an enlightened teacher, and if you applied the methods according to schedule, then you will get the appropriate feedback from your experiences."

Lü asked:

"What methods should be used and what kinds of schedules should be applied in the different stages of training?"

Chung said:

"There are twelve programs of training that should be practiced in sequence. They are the following: introducing yin and yang to each other, gathering and disseminating fire and water, mating the dragon and the tiger, heating and refining the medicines of the pill, ejecting the golden sparks from behind the navel, returning the jade elixir to the tan-t'iens, using the jade elixir to refine the body, returning the golden elixir to the tan-t'iens, using the golden elixir to refine the body, moving the refined vapor to the primordial regions, internal observation and exchanging the mundane for the sacred, and transcendence and emanating in different forms.

"You should attend to the following schedules diligently. First, follow the timing of the rise and fall of yin and yang yearly. Second, follow the numerics of the waxing and waning of the sun and the moon monthly. Third, each day is ruled by the four cardinal directions of the pa-k'ua. Therefore you will also need to follow the schedule of the ten celestial stems and the twelve terrestrial branches in the one hundred hours and the six thousand minutes. Review what you have done after each day of practice. Continue to do this until the day you shed your shell and ascend to immortality. Make sure that you do not make mistakes. Even from the beginning you should ignore all questionable techniques and try to apply your cultivation to daily life.

"When you collect the medicine, you will be filled with the golden essence of generative energy. At this time the mind must be prepared to conquer the yin ghosts. First, when the heart channel opens, you will feel something thrusting upward and your mouth will be filled with sweet fluid. Next yin and yang will interact and you will hear sounds of wind and thunder in your belly. Next the spirit and soul will stir and you may experience fearful images in your dreams. Next you will feel discomfort in the six bowels and the four limbs. Then you will discover that minor illnesses will go away naturally. Next the tan-t'ien will feel warm and your complexion will become clear and healthy. Next you will see numinous lights when you are in a dark room. Next, in your dreams you will feel strong and invulnerable; nothing can harm you and no one can hurt you. You will also feel as if you were carrying your child home. Next the golden gate will be locked securely and you will not lose your generative energy in your sleep. Next you will hear a crack of thunder. All your joints will be open and perspiration will pour from your body. Next the jade elixir will coagulate into a sticky sweet fluid. Next the luminous fluid will become a creamy substance. The fluid will gradually fill the mouth and then flow down to the belly. Next the bones will become light and the body will be ready to house the yang spirit. Your gait will be soft and you will be able to run like swift horses. Next your mind will not be stirred by the external environment, because all desires have disappeared. Next you will be able to transfer vapor out of your body and cure others of illness. Next the internal gaze will be clear and bright and will never grow dark. Next the eyes will be sharp and clear, hair will regenerate, and the aged will become young again. Next the true vapor will be plentiful and you will never feel hungry. You will need to eat only a little and you will not feel the effects of alcohol. Next the body will shine with a golden glow. Awareness is enhanced, and you will begin to feel the taste of the sacred pill in your mouth. The fragrance of the numinous elixir will penetrate the body, and its unique scent will linger in your mouth and nostrils. Even people around you will feel the effects. Next you will be able to scrutinize the details of things a hundred paces away. Next all scars will disappear and mucus and sweat will not flow from the body. Next, when the fetus matures, you will be filled with vapor and will not feel hunger. Next the intention will be clear and bright and will be compatible with the Great Void. All emotions and attachments will disappear from the mind. Below, you will be rid of the nine worms; above, you will slay the three monsters. Next, when the spirit and soul are able to journey to other realms, you will not need to sleep and you will be energetic day and night. Next the essence of yang will materialize. The house of the spirit will be firm and the body will not feel cold or heat. Next, matters of life and death will not bother you. In the stillness of internal observation, you will travel to the paradise of the immortal lands. Music will flow from the terraces of palaces and you will experience beauty beyond the imagination of mortals. Next, when you have accumulated enough merit and have repaid all karmic debts, you will be registered in the records of the three pure realms. You will be able to see changes in yin and yang, predict events happening in the realm of humanity, and see imminent disasters and blessings. Next you will be tired of the dust of the world and of its comings and goings. You will want to find a quiet place where you can purify yourself and let the immortal fetus emerge. When multiple bodies emanate from your body, you will know that you have entered the realm of the sacred. Next the true vapor will become purely yang, and in one single breath you will be able to collect the external mercury. Next the immortal fetus will want to exit the body and fly around, and you will see a bright light hovering inside your meditation room. Next, in stillness you will hear celestial music. When you encounter mortals, you will detect their pungent smells, even from those who are wealthy and noble. This is because mortals carry with them the pungent smell of the mundane. Next you will be able to change your appearance at will. Your body will be like that of a jade tree, your appearance will take on the air of an immortal, and your bones will emanate a golden glow. Next, wherever you go, you will receive sacred invitations and be visited by sacred beings. You will be able to command everything with one small movement of your hand. Whatever you want to happen will happen. Next, in stillness you will see purple clouds. A golden aura will also surround your body. Next the fire dragon will leap from your body or the mysterious crane will fly out of it. This indicates that your spirit has transcended the mundane shell and you are ready to be liberated from your body. After you have been liberated from the body, you will be enveloped by clouds of many colors. Harmonious vapors will circle around you; flowers will fall on you like rain; a pair of mysterious cranes will fly toward each other; fragrant scents will fill the air as the jade lady immortals descend toward you. In a solemn and grand ceremony, you will be given the purple writ of the celestial books and immortal regalia. Immortals will appear to your left and right and you will be escorted to return to Peng-lai. You will meet the Lord of Tzu-wei star in the Purple Palace, where your name and place of birth will be entered into the registers. According to the merits that you have accumulated, you will be given a home in the three islands. At this point your cultivation is complete, and you are truly an immortal."

Lü said:

"Today I have been fortunate to have received your teachings and to have heard the most subtle and mysterious principles of the secret workings of heaven and earth. Not only are my ears and eyes cleared, but my spirit has been renewed. My body has found a refuge, and I know that I am raised above the dirt and the feces. However, not everyone who knows the methods will be able to practice them, and not everyone who practices will succeed. The teachings concern matters of life and death, and time passes swiftly. If we do not know how to practice, we will never succeed. As such, we will be no different from those who are ignorant of the methods. Please tell me the schedules of the interactions, the methods that we should use, and how to practice them."

Chung said:

"There is a text titled *Ling-pao pi-fa* (Scripture of the Definitive Methods of the Precious Spirit). In it are ten chapters covering sixteen programs of training. Each chapter has six sections: the golden advice, the jade writ, sayings from the true origin, examples, the true mnemonics, and the main principles. The text discusses the Great Tao and describes the three purities. It tells us that the principles of cultivation are based on the rise and the fall of yin and yang in the sky and the earth, and that the applications are modeled after the waxing and waning of the essences of the sun and the moon. It contains the teachings of the five immortals on the three paths of cultivation. When the appropriate time comes, I will transmit those teachings to you."

The immortal Hun-fang (Cloud Chamber) [the Taoist name of Chungli Ch'uan] obtained these three volumes of the Ling-Pao (Precious Spirit) Scriptures in a cave in the Chung-nan Mountains. The first volume is titled "Golden Advice of the Primal Beginning"; the second volume is titled "Jade Writ of the Three Kings"; and the third volume is titled "The Commentaries of the True Origin of the Most High." Originally there were thousands of chapters, but these scrolls have been compiled into one volume of "definitive methods." In it are sixteen programs of training and six sections of commentaries. They explain that within yang there is yin and within yin there is yang. They describe the principles of the rise and fall of vapors in the sky and the earth. They tell us that water emerges from vapor and vapor emerges from water. They discuss the workings of the interaction of the heart and the kidneys. They tell us that in applying the principles of the eight trigrams to the twelve segments of the day, the key lies in the trigram ken. In tossing the tan-t'iens, the key is in the ni-wan

(Mud Ball) cavity. They even use examples of swallowing the breath and drawing in the fluid to illustrate how you should practice. However, the true teachings of cultivating the true vapor can only be transmitted orally and are not available in writing.